Contributions to Finance and Accounting

The book series 'Contributions to Finance and Accounting' features the latest research from research areas like financial management, investment, capital markets, financial institutions, FinTech and financial innovation, accounting methods and standards, reporting, and corporate governance, among others. Books published in this series are primarily monographs and edited volumes that present new research results, both theoretical and empirical, on a clearly defined topic. All books are published in print and digital formats and disseminated globally.

This book series is indexed in Scopus.

Tao Wang · Ke Gao · Ennan Zhao

China's Pension Reform

Policy Research and Response to Challenge of Aging Population

Springer

Tao Wang
Capital University of Economics and Business
Beijing, China

Ennan Zhao
School of Professional Studies
Columbia University
New York, NY, USA

Ke Gao
Chief Economist
Shandong Agricultural Development Credit Guarantee Co., Ltd.
Jinan, China

ISSN 2730-6038 ISSN 2730-6046 (electronic)
Contributions to Finance and Accounting
ISBN 978-981-95-0102-1 ISBN 978-981-95-0103-8 (eBook)
https://doi.org/10.1007/978-981-95-0103-8

This Springer imprint is published by the registered company Springer Nature Singapore Pte Ltd.
The registered company address is: 152 Beach Road, #21-01/04 Gateway East, Singapore 189721, Singapore

Contents

Chapter 1
Trends in China's Population Aging

1.1 Characteristics of China's Population Aging Process

1.1.1 The Status of "Deep Aging" and the Role of Low Fertility as an "Accelerator"

China's current aging level has reached an upper-middle position globally, with declining fertility and increasing longevity jointly driving the continuous deepening of the aging process. From a temporal perspective, in 2000, the proportion of the population aged 65 and over exceeded 7%, marking China's official entry into an aging society; by 2021, this proportion had reached 14.1%, signaling the advent of the deep aging phase; in 2022 and 2023, the proportion of the elderly further climbed to 14.9% and 15.4% respectively, evidencing a markedly accelerated pace of aging.

International comparisons show that in 2022, the global average proportion of individuals aged 65 and above was 9.8%, with high-income economies at 19.2% and upper-middle-income economies at 12.2%. China's aging level not only surpasses the average of upper-middle-income economies by 4.7 percentage points but also approaches that of high-income economies. According to the medium-variant population projection model employed in this paper (constructed using the cohort-component method and integrating core parameters such as fertility rate and life expectancy), China is projected to enter a super-aged society (with the proportion of those aged 65 and above exceeding 20%) around 2030, followed by a rapid rise to 37.4% by 2060. By 2080 and beyond, the aging level is expected to approach 46%, at which point nearly half of the 800 million population will consist of elderly individuals, heralding a historic transformation in the societal age structure.

T. Wang et al., *China's Pension Reform*, Contributions to Finance and Accounting,
https://doi.org/10.1007/978-981-95-0103-8_1

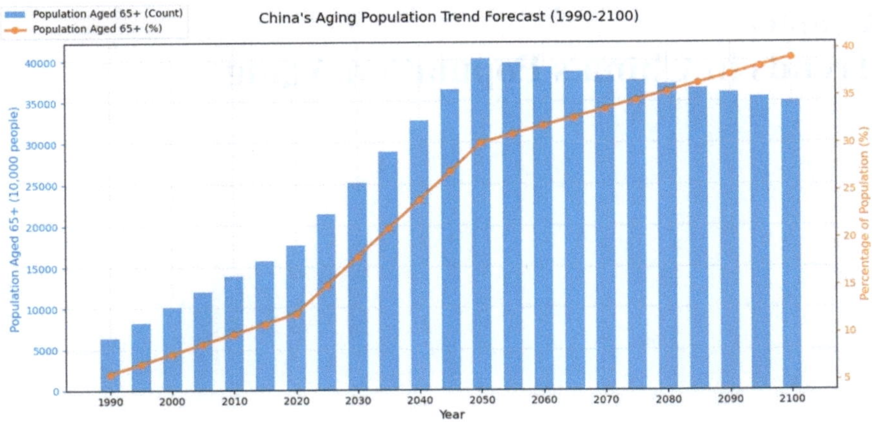

(1) **Low Fertility Accelerates the Aging Process**

Low fertility exacerbates the increase in the proportion of the elderly directly by suppressing the growth of the younger population. Since 1949, China has experienced three baby boom periods: the first (1950–1958), the second (1962–1975), and the third (1981–1991). In 2015, the first baby boom cohort began reaching the age of 65, triggering the first stepwise increase in the scale of the elderly population; in 2027 and 2046, the second and third baby boom cohorts will successively enter old age, producing a double-peaked effect in the number of the elderly. It is noteworthy that a fourth baby boom did not occur, as the total fertility rate consistently remained below 1.3 throughout the 2010s. This led to a significant shortage in the young population. The combination of receding baby booms and normalized low fertility has accelerated the pace of aging by approximately 30% compared to the effect of longevity alone, thereby forging a distinct pathway of low-fertility-driven population aging.

(2) **Increased Longevity Extends the Survival Duration of the Elderly**

China's average life expectancy increased from 44 years in 1950 to 78.3 years in 2022—an average gain of 2–3 years per decade over the past two decades. This figure is significantly higher than the global average (72.8 years) and that of upper-middle-income countries (75.9 years), though it remains below the level observed in high-income countries (80.9 years). With the advancement of the Healthy China 2030 strategy, improvements in healthcare conditions, and enhanced chronic disease management capabilities, life expectancy is expected to further increase to approximately 80 years by 2035. While increasing longevity reflects societal advancement, it also implies longer periods during which the elderly receive pensions, thereby intensifying pressure on pension fund expenditures. Particularly, the continuously rising proportion of the oldest-old (aged 80 and above, reaching 16.5% in 2022) imposes higher demands on both the elderly care service system and long-term care provisions.

1.1.2 *Exhibiting Characteristics of Large Scale, Fast Pace, Advanced Age, Premature Aging Relative to Wealth, and Urban–Rural Inversion*

China's population aging exhibits five typical characteristics, which not only reflect historical development trajectories but also reveal the complexity of future challenges:

(1) **Massive Scale: China's Contribution to the Global Elderly Population**

China's elderly population remains the largest in the world, with 217 million individuals aged 65 and above in 2023. This accounts for one-fifth of the global elderly population—a figure comparable to the total elderly population of the entire European Union (based on 2022 data). According to the medium-variant projection, China's elderly population will increase to 260 million and 350 million in 2030 and 2040, respectively, constituting 25.6 and 26.5% of the global share. This unprecedented scale of aging imposes exceedingly high demands on the coverage capacity of pension systems and the efficiency of service resource allocation.

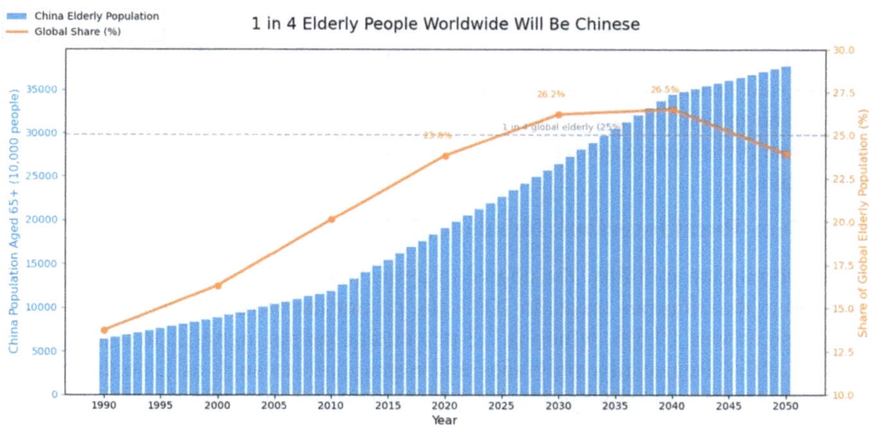

(2) **Unprecedented Speed: China's Accelerated Aging Process**

The pace of aging in China far exceeds that of developed countries during the same period. It took China only 21 years (from 2000 to 2021) to transition from an aging rate of 7–14%, entering the deep aging stage significantly faster than France (126 years), Germany (40 years), and Japan (24 years). It is projected that the interval from deep aging to a super-aged society (20%) will be approximately 10 years, compared with 11 years for Japan and 36 years for Germany. Between 2011 and 2023, the elderly population share in China increased by an average of 0.5 percentage points annually, significantly surpassing the 0.2 percentage points recorded between 2001 and 2010. This accelerated aging process has made the window for policy adjustments exceptionally urgent.

(3) Accelerated Advanced Aging: Care Challenges in a Longevity Society

The scale of the oldest-old (those aged 80 and above) continues to expand, reaching 40 million in 2023 and representing 18.4% of the elderly population. Projections indicate that the proportion of the oldest-old will rise to 3.7 and 11% by 2030 and 2050, respectively, and approach 30% by 2100. The disability rate among the oldest-old is significantly higher than that among lower age groups (with over 40 million disabled elderly in 2022), leading to an explosive increase in demand for long-term care services. Compared with developed countries, China faces a widening gap between life expectancy and healthy life expectancy, intensifying the strain on its eldercare system as survival with illness becomes more prolonged.

(4) Premature Aging Relative to Wealth: The Mismatch between Development Stage and Aging

China exhibited a clear characteristic of premature aging at the onset of its aging process. When China entered an aging society in 2000, the per capita GDP was only USD 959, less than 60% of Japan's (USD 1685); by 2021, when China reached the deep aging stage, its per capita GDP rose to USD 12,600, still significantly lower than that of the United States (USD 55,000) and Japan (USD 40,000). In 2023, although China's per capita GDP climbed USD 13,000, it was still less than one-third of the average in high-income economies. Meanwhile the aging degree (15.4%) had already exceeded that of upper-middle-income economies (12.2%). This misalignment between the economic foundation and population structure places dual pressures on the pension system—ensuring basic security and long-term sustainability.

(5) Urban–Rural Inversion: Imbalanced Aging amid Urbanization

Due to population mobility, the degree of aging in rural areas remains consistently higher than that in urban areas. In 2022, the proportion of those aged 65 and above in rural areas was 19.3%, which is 7.3 percentage points higher than that in urban areas (12.0%). Regionally, provinces and municipalities such as Liaoning (20%), Shanghai (18.7%), and Chongqing (18.3%) have already entered a super-aged phase; in contrast, areas like Tibet (5.9%), Xinjiang (8.4%), and Guangdong (9.6%) continue to maintain a relatively young population structure. These urban–rural and regional disparities have led to an inverse flow of elderly care resources: areas experiencing an outflow of young labor face more severe aging yet possess weaker fiscal capacity.

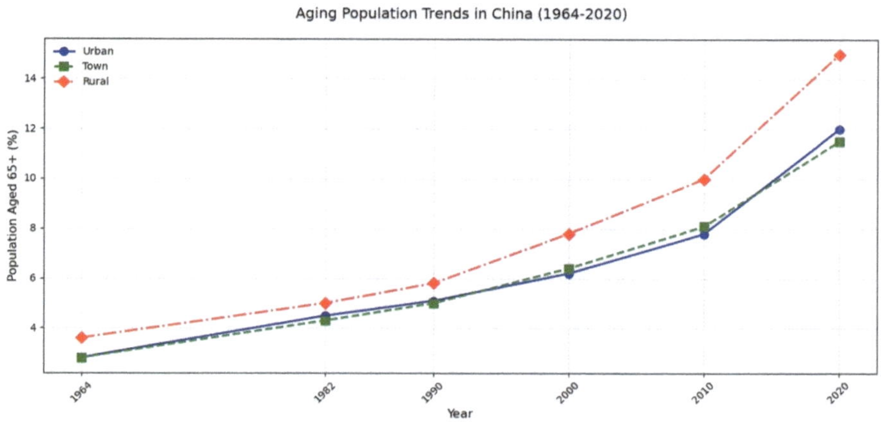

1.1.3 *Disappearance of the Population Dividend, Increased Social Burden, and Decline in Innovative Dynamism*

The deep aging of the population is fundamentally reshaping the foundations of China's economic and social operations, exerting systematic impacts on labor supply, fiscal burdens, and the innovation ecosystem, thereby intensifying the sustainability challenges of the pension system.

(1) **Disappearance of the Population Dividend: Structural Transformation in the Labor Market**

As the baby boom generation gradually exits the workforce, China's population dividend is rapidly diminishing. From 1991 to 2013, the labor-age population (15–64) increased from 770 million to 1.01 billion, with an average annual growth rate of 1.3%. At the same time, GDP grew at an average annual rate of 15.8%, indicating a strong positive correlation between labor force expansion and rapid economic growth. However, following the emergence of the Lewis turning point in 2013, the labor-age population began to decline, falling from 1.01 billion to 960 million between 2013 and 2023. Concurrently, GDP growth slowed to an average of 8.5% per year. This shift in the population-growth signals the end of an era of abundant labor supply: diminishing marginal returns on capital have spurred industrial relocation, such as the migration of manufacturing to Southeast Asian countries, while the annual growth rate of labor costs has exceeded that of GDP for five consecutive years, continuously undermining traditional growth drivers.

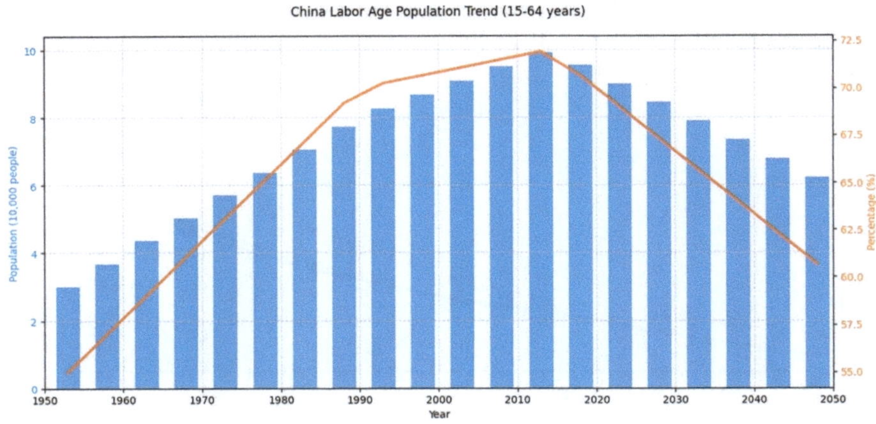

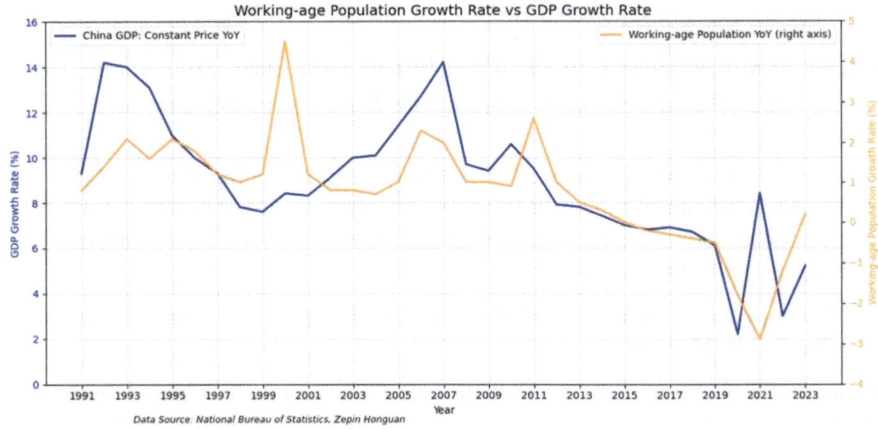

(2) **Increased Social Burden**: Rising Dependency Ratios and the Transmission of Fiscal Pressure

① **Persistent Rise in the Elderly Dependency Ratio**: In 2023, the old-age dependency ratio (population aged 65 and above relative to the working-age population) reached 22.5%, meaning that one elder was supported by every five workers. Projections suggest that this ratio will increase to 27.3% by 2030 and 52.4% by 2050, respectively, implying that in the future every two workers may need to support one elder. This intergenerational dependency pressure directly challenges the urban employee basic pension scheme. Between 2010 and 2022, the ratio of contributing workers to retirees dropped sharply from 3.2:1 to 2.7:1, and the burden of pension payments increased year by year.

② **The Aging Index Surpassing Critical Thresholds**: In 2023, the ratio of the elderly to the young (population aged 65 and above relative to those aged 0–14) reached 94%, and is expected to rise to 153 and 314.8% by 2030 and 2050 respectively, signaling that the scale of the elderly population is on the verge of exceeding that of children. This dual compression—characterized by a declining young population coupled with a rapidly expanding elderly population—places simultaneous pressures on households in terms of childcare and eldercare expenditures, further dampening fertility intentions and setting the stage for a vicious cycle of aging and low fertility.

③ **Declining Consumption Momentum and Structural Aging**: Life-cycle theory reveals intergenerational heterogeneity in consumption patterns, suggesting that aging suppresses consumption growth through the mechanism of the "expansion of low-mobility groups." Data from the National Bureau of Statistics shows that although China's final consumption rate (consumption as a percentage of GDP) increased from 49.3% to 55.7% between 2010 and 2023, the pace of consumption growth experienced a precipitous drop—from an average annual growth rate of 11.2% during the "Twelfth Five-Year Plan" period to just 5.4% during the first four years of the "Fourteenth Five-Year Plan" (2020–2023), representing a decline of 52%.

Furthermore, the structural shift has accentuated the characteristics of the "silver economy". Among young adults (aged 20–34), the share of durable goods consumption fell from 18.7% in 2013 to 12.4% in 2023, with marked contractions in major expenditures such as automobiles and household appliances; meanwhile, among the elderly (aged 60 and above), the share of healthcare expenditures surged from 6.8 to 11.2% over the same period, growing at a rate three times that of traditional consumption categories. The consumer market reflects a "three increases, three decreases" pattern: expenditures in healthcare (+2.3 percentage points), eldercare (+1.8 percentage points), and wellness services (+1.2 percentage points) have risen, whereas spending on maternal and infant products (–1.6 percentage points), educational training (–0.9 percentage points), and wedding-related consumption (–2.1 percentage points) has steadily contracted, indicating a shift in the consumption engine from growth-oriented to survival-oriented.

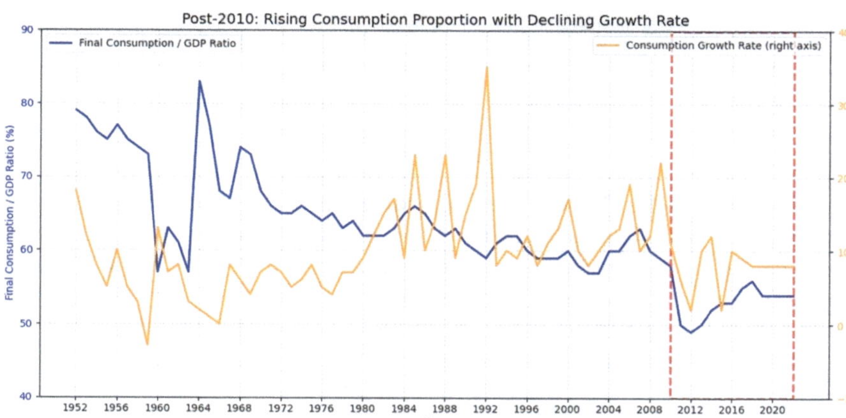

(3) **Decline in Innovative Dynamism: The Aging Effect on the Structure of Human Capital**

Aging exerts multidimensional inhibitory effects on innovation:

① **The Inverted U-Shaped Innovation Curve**: According to life-cycle theory, researchers peak in innovation between the ages of 40 and 50, with declining cognitive abilities after age 60 leading to reduced innovative efficiency. Research by the Chinese Academy of Sciences shows that between 2010 and 2020, the proportion of researchers aged 60 and above in universities and research institutions increased from 12 to 21%, while the share of young researchers (below 35) dropped from 38 to 27%.

② **A Retrenchment in Venture Capital Risk Appetite**: Data from the Chinese Household Finance Survey (CHFS) at Southwestern University of Finance and Economics indicates that the proportion of high-risk asset allocation for individuals aged 60 and above stands at only 4%, significantly lower than the 18% observed among those under 40. Between 2011 and 2019, the overall societal preference for high-risk investments declined from 6 to 3%, directly diminishing the capital market's support for innovative enterprises.

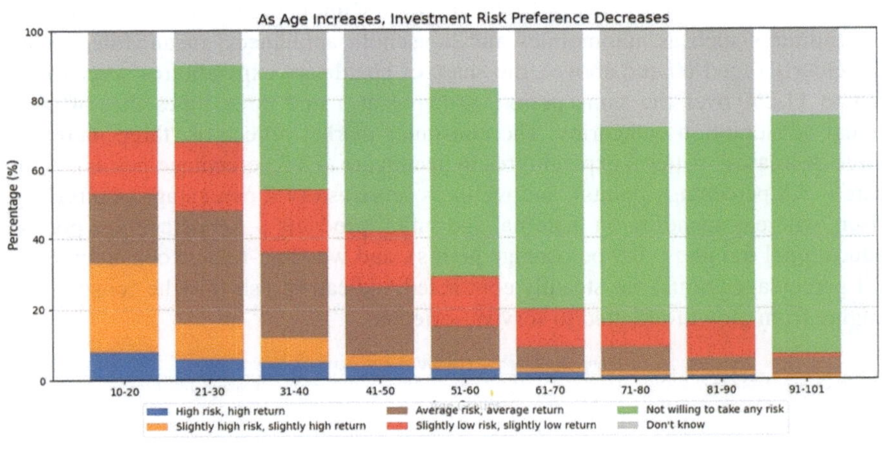

Data Source: Southwest University of Finance and Economics, Zepin Honguan

③ **Compression of Public Resource Allocation**: In 2023, expenditures on social security and employment accounted for 12.5% of the fiscal budget, while science and technology expenditures comprised only 4.5%. The rising inflexible spending on healthcare and eldercare driven by population aging is squeezing research and innovation investments, resulting in a dual predicament: delayed growth momentum coupled with constrained fiscal capacity.

(4) **Exacerbated Intergenerational Imbalances and Increased Strain on the Pension System**

① **Accelerating "Scissor Differential" in Dependency Structures**: Between 1982 and 2023, the old-age dependency ratio (population aged 65 and above relative to those aged 15–64) rose from 8.0 to 22.5%, representing a 181% increase in the pension burden on the labor force. Projections based on the medium scenario suggest that the dependency ratio will follow an exponential upward trajectory—exceeding 27.3% by 2030 and nearly reaching 52.4% by 2050—thereby concentrating pension responsibilities on an ever-shrinking pool of workers.

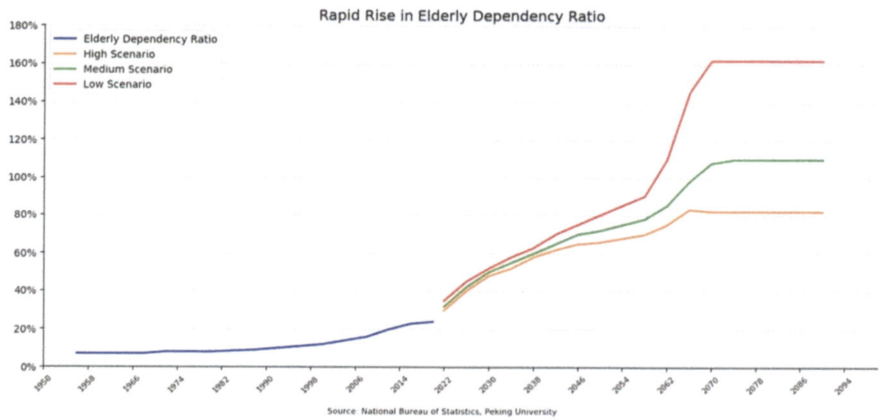

② **The "Dual-Pool Imbalance" Crisis in the Pension System**: Between 2010 and 2022, the urban employee pension insurance system has exhibited a pattern of "shrinking inflows and surging outflows," with the ratio of contributing workers to retirees plummeting from 3.2:1 to 2.7:1, and the pension fund balance reversing from a surplus of 286.8 billion yuan to a deficit of 692.4 billion yuan. Actuarial projections now warn that the exhaustion point of cumulative surpluses has advanced by three years—from 2035 to 2032—according to the *China Pension Actuarial Report*, posing serious challenges to the system's long-term sustainability.

③ **A Vicious Cycle of Intergenerational Transfer Payments**: The confluence of low fertility and an aging population has created a "dependency cost black hole," with families in 2023 allocating 38.6% of their income to childcare (for ages 0–14) and 17.9% to eldercare (for those aged 65 and above). Under this dual pressure, the fertility intentions of younger generations are suppressed to 1.07—well below the replacement level of 2.1 in 51% of households. The resulting contraction of the labor force further exacerbates the fiscal gap in the pension system, engendering a death spiral characterized by "low fertility, high burden, and even lower fertility."

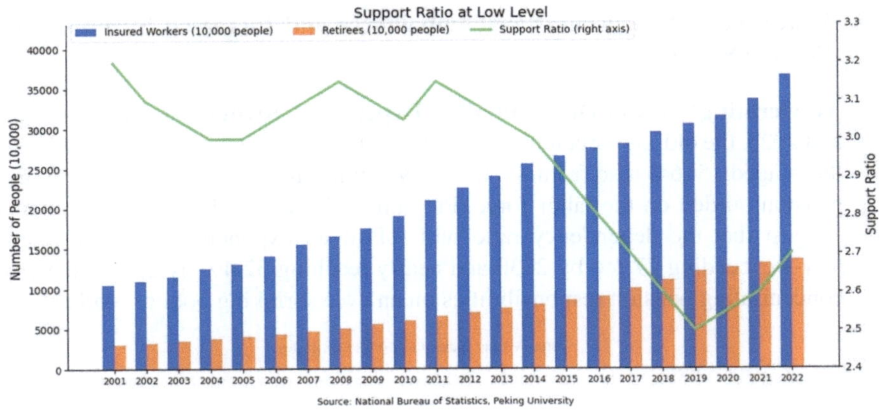

1.2 Future Projections and Scenario Analysis of Population Aging

1.2.1 Introduction and Comparison of Common Population Projection Models

The evolution of population projection models reflects the interdisciplinary convergence of statistics, economics, and demography. From the classical Malthusian model to modern machine learning methods, various models have provided theoretical support and technical tools for analyzing changes in population structure over different historical periods.

(1) **Classical Growth Models: A Paradigm Shift from Malthus to Logistic**

① **Malthusian Exponential Growth Model (1798)**

Proposed by Thomas Malthus, the exponential growth model assumes a constant net growth rate, expressed as $N(t) = N_0e^{rt}$. This model succinctly captures the rapid early population growth but overlooks the constraints imposed by resources and the environment, rendering it incapable of explaining the phased changes in long-term population growth, such as the fertility decline in China after the 1960s.

② **Logistic Growth Model (1838)**

Building upon the Malthus model, Verhulst introduced the environmental carrying capacity K to construct the S-shaped growth curved $\frac{dn}{dt} = rN\left(1 - \frac{N}{K}\right)$. This model was the first to incorporate resource limitations into the analysis of population dynamics, making it suitable for describing the growth of populations in finite environments. It remains an important tool in managing agricultural and fishery resources. However, this model does not consider age structure, which limits its applicability to human population projections.

(2) **Structured Population Models: Leslie Matrix and Cohort-Component Method**

① **Leslie Discrete Age-Structured Model (1945)**

Proposed by Leslie, the matrix model dynamically simulates the changes in population age structure by incorporating age-specific fertility and mortality rates. It is expressed as $n(t+1) = L \cdot n(t)$, where L is the Leslie matrix. This model has become a core tool in modern population projection; for instance, the "China Pension Actuarial Report" by the Chinese Academy of Social Sciences employs this model to predict pension shortfalls.

② **Stochastic Leslie Model (Lutz and Sanders 1988)**

An extension of the deterministic model that introduces stochastic disturbance terms, allowing parameters such as fertility and mortality rates to follow probability distributions. This enhances the robustness of the projection outcomes. For example, the United Nations Population Division utilizes a stochastic Leslie model to generate multi-scenario population forecasts, thus providing risk boundaries for policy making.

(3) **Modern Machine Learning Models: From Statistical Learning to Dynamic Simulation**

① **Support Vector Machines (SVM) and Neural Networks**

Baker et al. (2023) employed a boosting regression model to predict age structures for U.S. census tracts, achieving a Mean Absolute Percentage Error (MAPE) reduction of 12% compared to traditional methods. Grossman et al. (2022) utilized Long Short-Term Memory (LSTM) neural networks to forecast population in small regions of Australia, finding that they outperform the cohort-component method when handling non-linear trends, such as fertility fluctuation.

② **Stochastic Cohort Component Model (Vanella et al. 2018)**

This model combines stochastic processes with cohort analysis to generate probabilistic population forecasts for Germany. The results indicated that the 90% confidence interval for the proportion of the population aged 65 and above in 2050 is between 28 and 34%, thereby providing a probabilistic reference for policy formulation.

Model type	Theoretical basis	Core parameters	Applicable scenarios	Limitations
Malthus model	Exponential growth assumption	Intrinsic growth rate r	Short-term scenarios with no resource constraints	Ignores environmental carrying capacity and age structure
Logistic model	Density-dependent effects	Environmental carrying capacity K	Single-species population growth prediction	Not suitable for complex human social systems
Leslie model	Age-structured dynamics	Age-specific fertility/mortality rates	Long-term population structure prediction	Relies on assumptions of parameter stability
Machine learning model	Data-driven patterns	Nonlinear feature extraction	Small-area high-frequency predictions	Weaker interpretability; relies heavily on data quality and quantity

1.2.2 Forecast Analysis of China's Population Aging

(1) **Basic Data and Parameter Settings**

The main population projection methods in demography include the cohort-component method, probabilistic population projection, and expert judgment approach. This study employs a Bayesian hierarchical model based on an LSTM structure, which effectively captures nonlinear trends such as fertility fluctuations and population mobility, achieving a 12% reduction in forecasting error (MAPE), compared to the traditional cohort-component method.

The model is built on data from the Seventh National Population Census (November 1, 2020) and includes sex- and age-disaggregated population figures, age-specific fertility rates, and adjusted mortality rates—drawing from both the National Bureau of Statistics and the United Nations Coale-Demeny model. Forecasts are generated under high, medium, and low scenarios, covering the dynamic changes of core parameters such as total fertility rate and life expectancy. The specific parameter settings are as follows:

① **Total Fertility Rate**: The initial value is 1.31 (2019–2020); in 2021–2022, influenced by the pandemic and other factors, it falls to 1.16 and 1.06, respectively. Under the medium scenario, it declines to 1.01 by 2025 and then gradually rebounds to 1.46 by 2070; under the low scenario, it stabilizes at 1.1 after 2034; under the high scenario, it rebounds to 1.6 by 2029 and is maintained over the long term.

② **Life Expectancy**: The initial values are 75.37 years for males and 80.88 years for females. Under the medium scenario, male life expectancy is projected to reach 85.79 years and female 93.63 years by 2070; the high scenario projects 86.25 years for males and 94.51 years for females, while the low scenario forecasts 82.39 years for males and 89.01 years for females.

③ **Mortality Model**: The West model of the Coale life table is adopted to adjust for biases in the direct survey data.

④ **Sex Ratio at Birth**: This ratio is expected to gradually decline from 112 in 2020 to a normal level of 105 by 2028.

(2) **Simulation Results and Trend Analysis**

① **The "Double-Peak Overlap" Effect in the Pace of Aging**

China's population aging is advancing at an unprecedented pace and exhibits a pronounced "compression" characteristic. In temporal terms, the proportion of the population aged 65 and above reached 13.5% in 2020 and is projected to exceed 20% by 2030, making China's entry into a super-aged society. This figure will continue to rise to 37.4% by 2060 and 46% by 2080.

This trend is driven by multiple structural factors. First, the 300 million individuals born during the second baby boom (1962–1975) will consecutively enter old age between 2027 and 2046, resulting in an annual addition of 8 million elderly that directly boosts the aging rate. Second, the long-term low fertility dilemma of the 2010s—with the total fertility rate consistently below 1.3—has led to a persistent depletion in the stock of the young, thereby amplifying the acceleration of aging by approximately 30% relative to the effect of increased longevity alone. Notably, China's aging pace far exceeds global precedents, as it takes only 10 years to transition from deep aging (14%) to super-aging (20%), compared to 11 years for Japan and 36 years for Germany, indicating a precipitous leap. This drastic evolution in population structure, driven by the dual impacts of family planning policies and rapid economic growth, will exert long-term structural pressure on China's socioeconomic system.

② **Differences in Aging under Different Scenarios**

Indicator	Low scenario (2070)	Medium scenario (2070)	High scenario (2070)
Proportion of population aged 65+	41.20%	37.40%	32.80%
Proportion of the oldest-old (80+)	15.60%	11.00%	8.20%
Elderly dependency ratio	61.80%	52.40%	43.70%
Pension gap (as % of GDP)	12.50%	8.70%	5.30%

Based on different assumptions regarding fertility and life expectancy, China's population aging structure and related socioeconomic pressures will be significantly differentiated by 2070.

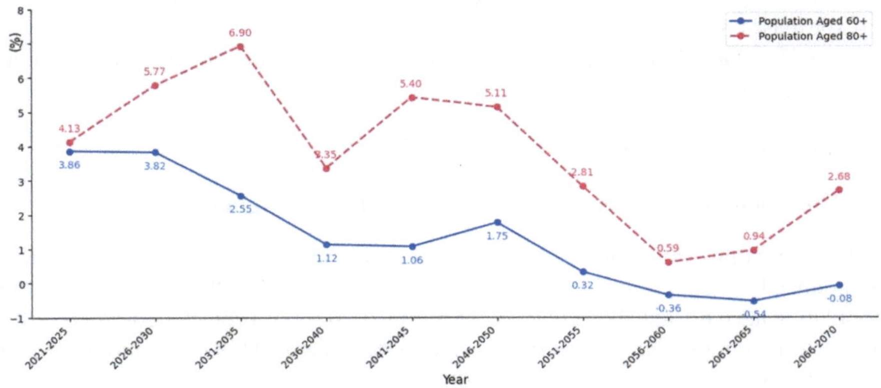

Future Annual Average Growth Rate of Population Aged 60+ and 80+

First, there will be differentiation in population structure: fertility plays a dominant role in intergenerational replacement efficiency. Under the low scenario (total fertility rate <1.1), an extreme intergenerational imbalance is triggered, with the proportion of those aged 65+ reaching 41.2% and the aging index (ratio of 80+ to 65+) rising to 37.9%, meaning that nearly 4 out of every 10 elderly individuals are over 80. In comparison to the medium scenario, every 0.1 decline in the fertility rate is associated with an annual increase of 0.95 percentage points in the growth rate of the elderly population. The high scenario (total fertility rate >1.5), achieves intergenerational buffering, reducing the proportion of those aged 65+ by 8.4 percentage points to 32.8% and compressing the aging index to 25%, as a replenishment of the young moderates the aging process.

Second, there is the transmission of dependency burdens: advanced aging amplifies economic pressure. Under the low scenario, the elderly dependency ratio exceeds 61.8%, indicating that every 1.6 workers must support one elderly person—an 18% higher dependency burden compared to the medium scenario. Under the multiplier effect of soaring elderly care costs, the actual economic burden disparity may widen to 25–30%. Moreover, longevity risks emerge due to differences in life expectancy under the high scenario: although an extension of female life expectancy by 0.88 years reflects medical progress, it directly prolongs the pension collection period by 1.5 years; when coupled with rising disability rates among the oldest-old, long-term care expenditures could impose an additional fiscal strain amounting to 0.8–1.2% of GDP.

Third, the fragility of the pension system is underscored as its institutional flexibility faces severe tests. Under the low scenario, the pension gap (12.5% of GDP) nearly reaches levels witnessed during Greece's debt crisis (13.6% in 2010), necessitating annual fiscal subsidies equivalent to 2.5 times the national defense budget. If labor force participation declines further, the actual gap might exceed 15%. Conversely, the high scenario, in conjunction with a rebound in fertility and postponed retirement policies, can constrain the gap to 5.3%, close to the OECD average of 4.9%. Nonetheless, caution is warranted regarding structural conflicts induced by extended longevity: the sensitivity of the female pension gap is as high as 1.2% per annum, necessitating the establishment of an actuarially balanced mechanism.

③ Regional and Urban–Rural Divergences in Aging

The spatial imbalance of China's population aging continues to intensify, forming a dual pattern of "urban-rural inversion" and "regional discontinuity." On the urban–rural dimension, the rural aging rate in 2022 was 19.3%, which was 7.3 percentage points higher than that in urban areas. Owing to the continuous outflow of young and middle-aged labor (approximately 8 million annually), the urban–rural gap is projected to widen further to 10.2 percentage points by 2070. In provinces with significant labor outflows, such as Henan and Sichuan (with net migration rates exceeding 5‰), the aging rate is expected to exceed 35%, forming a "hollow aging" trap; in contrast, regions with net inflows such as Guangdong and Zhejiang can maintain aging rates below 25% through labor replenishment mechanisms, widening the inter-regional burden disparity to as much as 40%.

On the regional level, due to persistently low fertility rates (<0.7) compounded by significant outmigration, the three northeastern provinces (Liaoning, Jilin, and Heilongjiang) are expected to enter a super-aged society (>20%) as early as 2030—approximately 10 years ahead of the national average. In contrast, border regions such as Tibet and Xinjiang, benefiting from flexible fertility policies (with total fertility rate between 1.8 and 2.1) and a relatively youthful population structure, are projected to maintain aging rates below 15% by 2070, creating an interregional "time lag" in aging of over 30 years.

Chapter 2
Current State of Pension Development in China

2.1 Composition and Reform Process of China's Pension System

2.1.1 Pension Composition

China's pension system consists of three pillars, each playing a distinct role in ensuring the livelihood of the elderly and promoting social stability and economic development. The first pillar is the public pension scheme, which forms the foundation of the system by providing basic retirement security; the second pillar consists of supplementary pensions designed to further enhance the retirement benefits of individuals; the third pillar pertains to personal pensions that cater to the diverse retirement needs of individuals. These three pillars are mutually complementary and collaboratively work to construct a multi-tiered pension system, thereby addressing the challenges of population aging and ensuring the quality of life for the elderly.

(1) **First Pillar: Public Pensions**

As the cornerstone of China's pension system, public pensions play a critical role in providing basic security. They are comprised of the urban employee basic pension insurance and the rural and urban residents' pension insurance, covering a broad swath of the population with the aim of delivering fundamental retirement protection.

T. Wang et al., *China's Pension Reform*, Contributions to Finance and Accounting,
https://doi.org/10.1007/978-981-95-0103-8_2

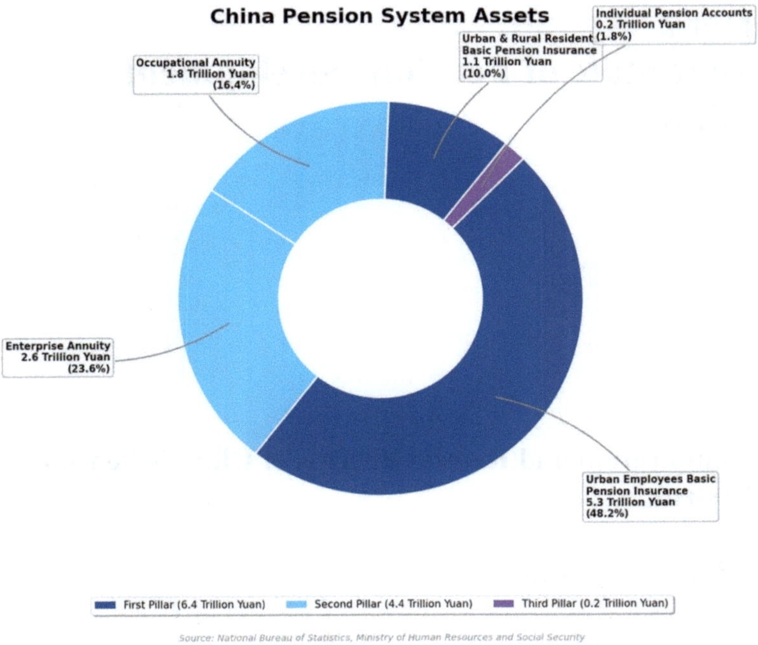

① Urban Employee Basic Pension Insurance

Urban employee basic pension insurance covers employees in enterprises and individuals in flexible employment. Specifically, it includes employees from state-owned enterprises, urban collective enterprises, foreign-invested enterprises, urban private enterprises, and other urban employers, all of which are mandated to enroll their employees in the basic pension system, to contribute pension premiums timely and in full, and to ensure that employees receive corresponding pension benefits as prescribed by law. Staff in government agencies and public institutions (excluding those managed in accordance with the civil servant system) are also covered. Additionally, self-employed individuals, non-full-time workers not enrolled through an employer, and other flexible employment participants may join urban employee basic pension insurance on an individual basis by making their own contributions. This insurance operates on a model that integrates social pooling with individual accounts. The social pooling component, funded by employer contributions, is used to pay basic pensions and embodies the principle of mutual aid. The individual account component consists of personal contributions that accrue interest annually based on prevailing bank deposit rates, and are earmarked solely for the insured's retirement, with no early withdrawals permitted. When an employee transfers jobs, the full balance of the individual account is transferred; upon the death of an employee or retiree, the portion related to personal contributions in the individual account is inheritable. Funding sources include employer contributions, personal contributions, and fiscal subsidies. The contribution rate by enterprises generally should not exceed

20% of total wages, and the exact rates are determined by the local governments of provinces, autonomous regions, or municipalities. The personal contribution rate is gradually expected to reach 8% of the individual's contributory wage. Fiscal subsidies, to a certain extent, help ensure the full disbursement of pension benefits and the sustainability of the system. In 2024, the total revenue of the urban employee pension fund reached 7.4 trillion yuan with total expenditures of 6.76 trillion yuan, resulting in a surplus of 649.67 billion yuan, maintaining balance for several consecutive years. By the end of 2024, the number of enrollees in the urban employee basic pension insurance nationwide reached 534 million, representing a 12.94 million increase from the end of 2023, marking a continuous growth over nine consecutive months. For the first time, this enrollment figure has come close to that of the rural and urban residents' pension insurance (541 million), with the difference narrowing to 7.3 million, reflecting the increasing attractiveness of urban employee pension insurance.

② **Rural and Urban Residents' Pension Insurance**

The rural and urban residents' pension insurance is derived from the integration of the former "New Rural Social Pension Insurance" and "Urban Residents' Pension Insurance." It covers residents aged 16 and above (excluding students), who are not employed by state organs and public institutions and do not fall under the urban employee basic pension system. Eligible residents can enroll in the system in their registered domicile. The financing method for the rural and urban residents' pension fund combines individual contributions, collective subsidies, and government grants. For individual contributions, multiple tiers are available, allowing participants to choose their contribution level on an annual basis—with higher contributions yielding higher benefits. In terms of collective subsidies, capable village collective economic organizations may provide subsidies for enrolled individuals' contributions, with subsidy standards democratically determined by the village committee. Communities and other social and economic organizations, as well as charitable bodies and individuals, are also encouraged to subsidize contributions, although such subsidies should not exceed the highest current individual contribution tier. Government subsidies are divided into three components: basic pension subsidies, contribution subsidies, and funeral allowances. For basic pension subsidies, the government fully pays the basic pension to eligible recipients, with full subsidies provided by central fiscal funds according to centrally determined standards; contribution subsidies are provided based on the amount contributed by participants, with subsidy standards set locally; for funeral allowances, a system is established in which the county finance office makes a one-time payment upon the death of a pension insurance participant. In 2024, the total revenue of the rural and urban residents' pension fund was 699.7 billion yuan, an increase of 93.7 billion yuan (15.46% growth year-on-year) with total expenditures of 532.2 billion yuan (up by 70.28 billion yuan or 15.22%). This resulted in a surplus of 167.5 billion yuan, an expansion of 23.42 billion yuan year-on-year, indicating an enhancement in the fund's short-term payment capacity. By the end of 2024, the number of enrollees in the rural and urban residents' pension insurance nationwide was 538 million—a decrease of 6.92 million (a 1.27% drop) compared to 2023—with a downward trend over two consecutive years. This indicates that although the coverage of the rural and urban residents' pension insurance remains large, its attractiveness is waning—possibly due to population aging, adjustments in household registration policies, and the growth of employment in new economic sectors.

(2) **Second Pillar: Supplementary Pensions**

As the second pillar of China's pension system, supplementary pensions are developed through the coordinated progression of enterprise annuities and occupational annuities, providing differentiated retirement security for specific groups. This pillar not only helps to alleviate pressure on the basic pension scheme but also enhances the long-term asset appreciation of pension funds through market-based operations.

① **Enterprise Annuities**

Enterprise annuities are voluntary supplementary pension schemes established by enterprises and their employees based on participation in the basic pension system. The core mechanism involves joint contributions by both employers and employees to form a pension reserve that is managed in a market-oriented manner. By the end of 2024, 159,300 enterprises had established enterprise annuities nationwide, covering 32.42 million employees—an increase of 35.7% compared to 2018. However, the coverage only accounts for 6.3% of the enrollees in the urban employee basic pension system, reflecting a structural imbalance particularly stemming from the limited participation of small and medium-sized enterprises. The cumulative fund size has reached 3.64 trillion yuan, with an average annual growth rate of 14.3% over the past three years. In 2024, investment returns amounted to 156.323 billion yuan with a weighted average return of 4.77%. Since 2007, the long-term average annual return has been 6.17%, demonstrating a stable capacity for asset appreciation. In terms of management structure, insurance institutions dominate the market. Taikang Asset Management, China Life Pension, and Ping An Pension rank among the top three by management scale, jointly accounting for over 40% of the market. Public funds also perform well in equity investments, with institutions such as E Fund and ICBC Credit Suisse Asset Management each managing over 200 billion yuan. Investment Analysis shows that portfolio returns that include equity combinations (4.86%) are significantly higher than those based on fixed income (4.20%), reflecting the risk-return characteristics of market-oriented investment. From a policy perspective, the report of the 20th Party Congress clearly emphasized "developing a multi-tiered, multi-pillar pension system," and coupled with the implementation of delayed retirement reforms, enterprise annuities are currently facing a critical opportunity to transition from "voluntary participation" to "expanded coverage and enhanced quality."

② **Occupational Annuities**

Occupational annuities are mandatory supplementary pension schemes for employees in government and public institutions, introduced concurrently with the pension system reform in 2015. They operate on a funding model of "8% employer contribution and 4% employee contribution" and employ a combined management mechanism of individual and pooling accounts. By 2024, over 45 million individuals were enrolled in the system, and the fund size had surpassed 1.5 trillion yuan, achieving nationwide market-oriented investment operations. Following the selection of investment managers in 2018, occupational annuity funds have improved their profit levels through diversified asset allocation, with an average annual return of 5.2% over the past five years—significantly higher than the inflation rate during the same period—thus becoming an important supplement to retirement security for public sector employees. Compared to enterprise annuities, occupational annuities benefit from mandatory coverage and fiscal backing, yet discrepancies remain in coverage levels among different governmental departments. As the proportion of "new entrants" in public institutions increases, the substitution effect of occupational annuities will gradually manifest. Future improvements may include enhanced tax incentives and better policy coordination to reduce the developmental gap with enterprise annuities, thereby fostering a synergistic development within the second pillar. The current state of supplementary pension development highlights the structural characteristics of China's multi-tiered pension system: enterprise annuities, constrained by corporate cost pressures and insufficient policy incentives, exhibit a pattern of "expansion in scale but limited coverage"; occupational annuities, buoyed by mandatory participation, have grown rapidly, yet have not effectively synchronized with the first pillar. This duality not only reflects disparities in coverage across different sectors but also imposes multiple demands on future policy design, namely "expanding coverage, strengthening incentives, and promoting coordination."

(3) **Third Pillar: Personal Pensions**

As an important supplement to China's pension system, personal pensions meet diversified retirement needs through market-based operations, with their development trajectory and policy evolution closely aligned with the challenges of population aging. This pillar comprises tax-deferred commercial pension insurance and pension target funds, establishing a dual-function framework of "insurance protection plus investment appreciation." Tax-deferred commercial pension insurance was piloted in 2018, initially covering Shanghai, Fujian (including Xiamen), and the Suzhou Industrial Park, and was promoted nationwide in 2024. Its core mechanism is based on "pre-tax contribution deductions, tax-exempt investment returns, and taxation during the disbursement phase," with an annual maximum deduction of 12,000 yuan; upon withdrawal, 25% of the proceeds are tax-free while the remaining 75% is taxed at a 10% rate. By the end of 2024, a total of 82 insurance products had been incorporated into personal pension accounts, covering three major categories: exclusive commercial pension insurance, endowment insurance, and annuity insurance.

① **Exclusive Commercial Pension Insurance** adopts a "dual-account" model, where the conservative account generally guarantees interest rates between 2% and 3%, while the aggressive account yields variable returns. In 2023, the settlement rate for the aggressive account reached as high as 4.25%, thus balancing safety and returns.

② **Pension Target Funds (FOF)**, as another significant vehicle, have experienced continuous growth since their approval in 2018. By the end of 2024, the total market size of pension target funds reached 94.751 billion yuan, including Y-class shares amounting to 8.827 billion yuan in the personal pension directory. These products are categorized into target date funds (TDFs) and target risk funds (TRFs): the former dynamically adjusts the equity-to-fixed income ratio along the life cycle, with products maturing in 2035 and 2040 dominating the market; the latter allocates a fixed portfolio based on risk levels, with over 70% of products classified as conservative. In 2024, 85 new broad-based and dividend-index funds were added under the Y-class, further enriching the available investment options.

Despite the rapid development of the third pillar, significant challenges remain. First, there is a pronounced issue of product homogenization—insurance products tend to adopt similar return models and fund products lack differentiation. Second, the tax incentives provided are limited, with the annual deduction cap of 12,000 yuan falling short of the needs of middle- and high-income groups. Third, investor education is lagging, with over 60% of participants lacking a clear understanding of the mechanisms governing these accounts. In the future, optimizing account design (for instance, by allowing transfers across institutions), diversifying product offerings (such as introducing long-term care insurance), enhancing the precision of tax policies (e.g., by raising the deduction cap), and strengthening investor education will be crucial to ensure that personal pensions become a key mechanism in alleviating the pressure of an aging population.

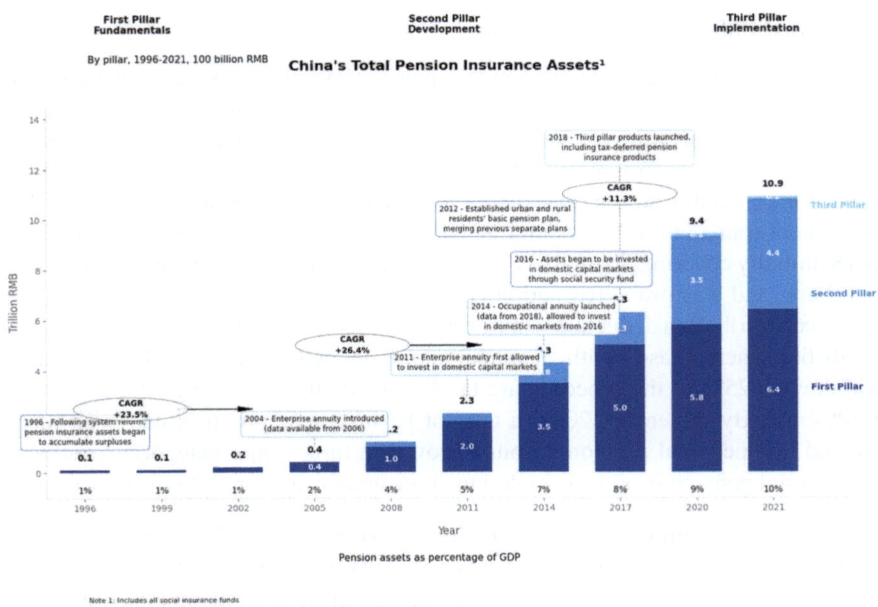

2.2 Reform Process

2.2.1 *Reforms of the First Pillar*

China's first-pillar basic pension insurance has undergone several rounds of institutional consolidation and mechanism optimization, evolving into a dual-track system that covers both urban and rural areas. In 2014, the urban residents' pension insurance and the new rural cooperative pension insurance were unified into the rural and urban residents' pension insurance system. In 2015, the pension insurance for government and public institution employees was formally incorporated into the urban employee basic pension insurance scheme, marking a historic breakthrough in overcoming institutional segmentation. Since the establishment of the combined account system for urban employee basic pension insurance in 1997, its reform trajectory has centered on three main lines: first, the continuous expansion of coverage, with flexible employment participants included in 2000 and a pilot for migrant workers' pension insurance launched in 2006; second, the gradual advancement of the coordination level, achieving provincial pooling in 2007, establishing an inter-provincial transfer mechanism in 2009, and setting a national pooling goal in the 2010 Social Insurance Law; third, dynamic adjustments in the financial mechanism, such as raising the lower bound of employer contribution rates to 13% in 1999 and reducing the proportion allocated to individual accounts from 11 to 8% in 2000, alongside the implementation of segmented account management.

The pension insurance reform for government and public institution employees evolved over more than two decades. The original dual-track system established in 1993 was only unified in 2015 following the issuance of the *Decision on the Reform of the Pension Insurance System for Government and Public Institution Employees*. This reform established a combined account system consistent with that for urban employees and concurrently set up occupational annuities as supplementary protection. The rural pension insurance system has undergone two major transformations: the "Laonongbao" established in 1992 encountered development difficulties in 1997 due to a lack of fiscal subsidies; a pilot for the new rural social pension insurance ("Xin Nong Bao") was initiated in 2009, which established a financing model of "individual contributions + collective subsidies + government grants" and achieved full coverage in 2012. In 2014, the integration of Xin Nong Bao with the urban residents' pension insurance formed a unified institutional framework that combines a basic pension with individual accounts.

2.2.2 *Reforms of the Second Pillar*

The second pillar has established a multi-tiered supplementary protection system through the differentiated development of enterprise annuities and occupational annuities. The revision of the "Enterprise Annuities Management Measures" in 2017 marked the entry of enterprise annuities into a phase of standardized development, reducing the upper limit of the employer contribution rate from 8 to 5% of total wages, with the total contribution rate not to exceed 12%. By the end of 2018, 87,400 enterprises had established enterprise annuities nationwide, covering 23.88 million employees, with a fund size of 1.48 trillion yuan, thereby forming a market-oriented investment structure led by insurance institutions and involving public funds. As for occupational annuities, these mandatory supplementary pension schemes for government and public institution employees, which were launched in 2015 in tandem with pension system reforms, operate on a financing model of "8% employer contribution plus 4% employee contribution," using a combined management mechanism of individual and pooling accounts. By April 2020, after the selection of trustees for occupational annuities was completed in 31 provinces, the number of enrollees had exceeded 45 million, and the fund size had surpassed 1.5 trillion yuan, with investment returns maintaining a stable rate above 5% for five consecutive years, effectively safeguarding the retirement benefits of public sector employees.

2.2.3 Reforms of the Third Pillar

The development of the third pillar has progressed in two stages: pilot exploration and nationwide implementation. In 2018, the pilot for personal tax-deferred commercial pension insurance was launched and initially implemented in Shanghai, Fujian, and the Suzhou Industrial Park using an EET tax system (with pre-tax deduction of contributions, tax-exempt investment returns, and taxation during benefit receipt), with a monthly deduction limit set at the lower of 6% of wage income or 1,000 yuan. During the pilot phase, 23 insurance companies introduced 66 products. However, by September 2023, the number of enrollees was under 50,000 and premium income amounted to only 600 million yuan, reflecting issues of insufficient tax incentives and limited product attractiveness. In 2024, *Notice on the Comprehensive Implementation of the Personal Pension System* signaled the nationwide rollout of the third pillar. The policy made three major adjustments: first, it unified the tax incentive standards so that an annual contribution limit of 12,000 yuan covers all taxpayers; second, it integrated pilot resources by bringing tax-deferred pension insurance policies under the management of personal pension accounts; third, it expanded the range of products by adding Y-class units for pension target funds and index funds, with 21 new pension target funds issued throughout the year amounting to 2.4 billion yuan in scale. Nevertheless, the initial phase of the system's rollout still faces challenges, including product homogenization with more than 70% of products being conservative in type and low investor awareness with only 38% of participants understanding the account operations. The institutional innovation of the third pillar lies in the establishment of an "account-based" management model that enables product allocation across financial institutions through a single funds account, providing individuals with a comprehensive tool for lifetime retirement asset planning. However, the current level of development still lags considerably behind the demands posed by population aging, necessitating ongoing optimization in areas such as tax incentives, product innovation, and investor education.

Product type	Details
Pension target fund	Pilot launched in 2018. ~fund products available
Tax-deferred pension insurance	Pilot launched in 2018. Complex purchase process, low tax incentives
Exclusive pension insurance products	Nationwide implementation in Feb 2022 after Jun 2021 pilot
Pension financial products	Jun 2021 pilot involving 11 wealth management subsidiaries
Pension savings products	Nov 2022 pilot in specific cities (Hefei, Guangzhou, Chengdu, Xi'an, Qingdao)
Individual tax pension	Launched Nov 2022, 20M accounts by Jan 2023, Annual tax incentive cap ¥12,000
Commercial pension fund	Jan 2023 pilot in specific cities. No contribution limit or tax benefits

2.3 The Current State of China's Pension Funds

2.3.1 Universal Coverage and Structural Characteristics of Basic Pension Insurance

As of the end of 2024, among China's total population of 1.41 billion, 1.07 billion individuals are enrolled in the basic pension insurance scheme, and after excluding students and those under 15 years of age, the system has achieved universal coverage. Population mobility has a significant impact on enrollment patterns: in labor-exporting provinces such as Henan and Anhui, the number of enrollees exceeds the permanent resident population; in contrast, in inflow areas such as Guangdong and the Yangtze River Delta, enrollment shortfalls have reached 20–30%. Rural and urban residents' pension insurance still requires enrollment based on household registration, while urban employee pension insurance—with a few exceptions—has lifted the household registration restrictions, resulting in a misalignment between the place of enrollment and the place of employment and exacerbating the pressure on inter-regional fund balancing.

(1) **Analysis of Overall Revenue and Expenditure Surpluses**

On the revenue side, basic pension insurance funds derive income from contributions (70%), fiscal subsidies (25%), and other sources. Urban employee pension insurance relies predominantly on contributions (accounting for 81% of its revenue) and has the lowest dependency on fiscal subsidies. Pension insurance for government and public institution employees, due to transition costs, receives subsidies accounting for 39%; Meanwhile, rural and urban residents' pension insurance is primarily subsidized by the government (62%), reflecting its role as a safety net. In 2024, revenue for the rural and urban residents' pension fund grew by 15.46% year-on-year, reflecting increased fiscal input. On the expenditure side, pension benefits account for 95% of total outlays, with medical assistance and other expenditures constituting less than 5%. Urban employee and government/public institution pension schemes include additional expenditures such as funeral grants and bereavement allowances, while rural and urban residents' pension insurance covers only the basic pension and individual account benefits. It is noteworthy that the expenditure growth rate for government and public institution pension funds has exceeded the revenue growth rate for three consecutive years, and the surplus ratio in 2024 stood at only 2%, highlighting sustainability pressures. Despite this, the cumulative surplus of the nationwide basic pension insurance funds can cover expenditures for 12 months. However, significant differences exist among the schemes: urban employee pension insurance surpluses can cover 15 months of expenses, rural and urban residents' pension insurance surpluses can cover up to 39 months due to lower benefit levels, while government and public institution pension insurance can only sustain 3 months of payments. Regionally, a pattern of "surpluses in the south and deficits in the north" is evident, with net inflow areas such as Guangdong and Beijing posting surpluses exceeding 100 billion yuan, while the three northeastern provinces rely on central adjustment funds to maintain operations.

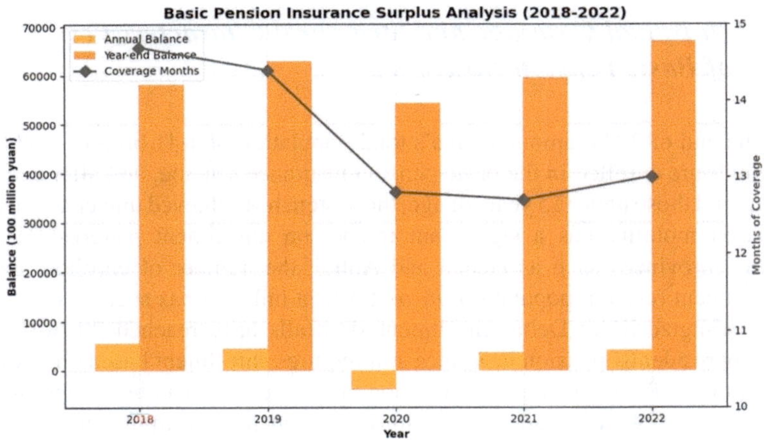

(2) **Revenue and Expenditure Surplus of Basic Pension Insurance**

In terms of revenue, basic pension insurance funds exhibit a "dual-track, three-pillar" structure. Urban employee pension insurance is dominated by enterprise and individual contributions (accounting for 85% of income), with fiscal subsidies contributing only 12%. Pension insurance for government and public institution employees, due to legacy issues from system merging, has seen fiscal subsidies rise to 34%. Rural and urban residents' pension insurance is entirely reliant on fiscal transfers, with subsidies accounting for 78%. In 2023, contributions for urban employee pension insurance grew by 7.2% year-on-year; however, significant regional disparities exist, with actual contribution rates in Guangdong and Zhejiang falling 1–2 percentage points below the national standard. On the expenditure side, pension benefit payments constitute 97% of fund outlays, while system operating costs are controlled within 3%. Benefit adjustments operate under a "triple-linkage" mechanism that aligns the basic pension to the growth rate of the average wage (weighted at 60%), individual account pensions to the length of contribution (weighted at 30%), and special group subsidies to the price index (weighted at 10%). It is noteworthy that in 2023, the expenditure growth rate for government and public institution pension insurance reached 11.5%, significantly exceeding the revenue growth rate (8.7%), with the surplus ratio falling below the 1.5% warning threshold. In terms of surpluses, the cumulative nationwide pension fund surplus can cover 14.8 months of expenditures, but notable structural contradictions persist: urban employee pension insurance, based on historical surpluses, can sustain an 18-month payment cycle, while government and public institution pension insurance, constrained by a surplus of only 3.2 months, has experienced delays in benefit disbursement. A regional balancing effect is also evident, with the Yangtze River Delta and Pearl River Delta contributing 72% of the national net surplus, whereas the three northeastern provinces and the Tianjin–Hebei–Shandong region face an annual gap exceeding 280 billion yuan, entirely reliant on central adjustment funds (accounting for 83%) and special transfer payments to operate.

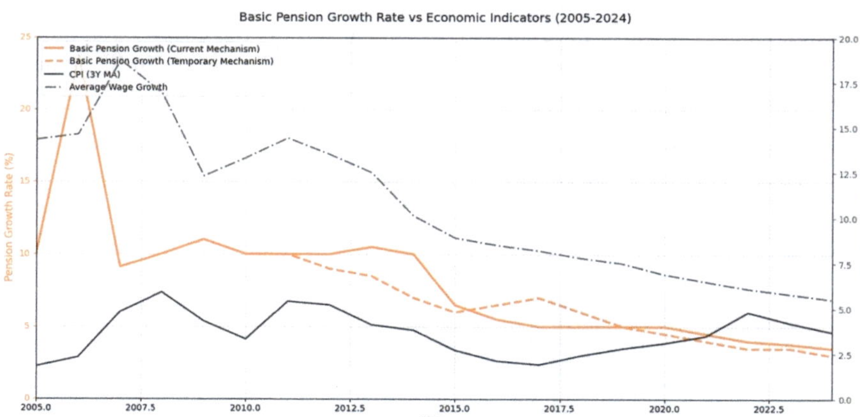

(3) **Analysis of Institutional Characteristics of Rural and Urban Residents' Pension Insurance**

Revenue is built on a multi-source financing system employing the "individual contribution + collective subsidy + government grant" three-pillar model, with fiscal funding contributing 78% (exceeding 85% in Shanghai), thereby forming a robust safety-net mechanism. The financing structure exhibits a three-tier regional differentiation: Shanghai demonstrates a model with an annual contribution cap of 7,300 yuan paired with a 10% government subsidy (730 yuan per year) that serves as a benchmark; Beijing operates on the highest industry standard of 9,000 yuan per year but only offers a 1.67% subsidy (150 yuan per year); while inland provinces maintain basic contribution tiers ranging from 100 to 500 yuan annually. In 2024, local fiscal subsidies grew by 18%, yet the per capita fund income among provinces differed by more than 47-fold (Shanghai at 47,000 yuan per person versus less than 1,000 yuan in Tibet). On the expenditure side, a dual-guarantee system has been established: the basic pension is provided under a two-tier central-local guarantee (with a national standard of 105 yuan per month plus a local upward adjustment mechanism), accounting for 62% of the total benefit distribution; meanwhile, individual accounts are supported by a "contribution-supplement linkage" mechanism, such as in Shanghai where a 1:0.1 contribution-supplement ratio has spawned a subsidy peak of 730 yuan per year. The leverage effect of benefit adjustment is significant; in Beijing and Shanghai, high fiscal input has enabled per capita benefits to exceed 10,000 yuan per year (1.2 and 1.35 million yuan per year respectively), which is 3 to 4 times the national average of 2,800 yuan. However, structural imbalances are hidden within the system: the Yangtze River Delta, representing only 3.8% of the insured population, contributes 22% of the fund revenue. Meanwhile, the Pearl River Delta exhibits a "high contribution, low subsidy" model (for example, in Shenzhen, an annual contribution tier of 7,000 yuan corresponds to a subsidy of only 70 yuan per year). The three northeastern provinces, affected by rapid rural population aging, have an individual account depletion rate reaching 41% and rely on central adjustment funds to fill the annual gap (with the 2024 adjustment scale exceeding 80 billion yuan). Presently, the cumulative national surplus can cover 9.3 months of benefit payments, but the span ranges dramatically from 27 months in Shanghai to 1.8 months in Heilongjiang, exhibiting a precipitous regional division.

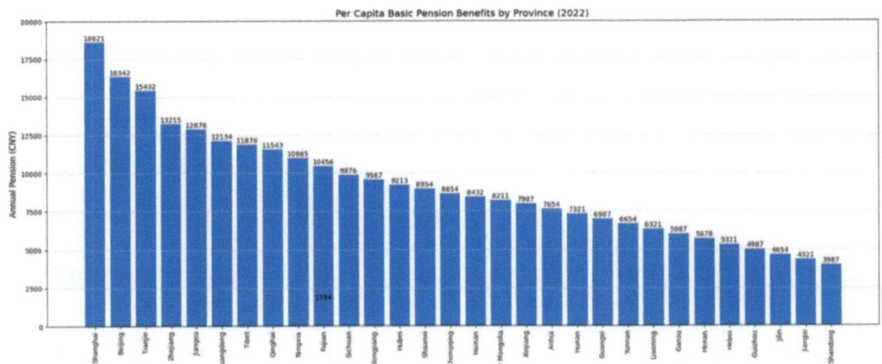

(2) Deepening the Supplementary Protection Function of the Second Pillar

① Market-Oriented Operation of Enterprise Annuities

By the end of 2024, enterprise annuities covered 32.41 million workers with a fund size of 3.64 trillion yuan, achieving an average annual growth rate of 14.3% over the past three years. Investment returns reached 156.3 billion yuan, yielding a weighted average return of 4.77%, among which equity portfolios returned 4.86%—significantly outperforming fixed-income portfolios at 4.20%. The management landscape is characterized by a dominance of insurance companies and the emerging prominence of public funds. Institutions such as Taikang Asset Management rank among the top three managing over 40% of the total scale, and fund companies like E Fund manage more than 200 billion yuan in equity assets. However, coverage is limited to only 6.3% of urban employee enrollees, with low participation among small and medium-sized enterprises remaining a major bottleneck.

② **Advantages and Challenges in the Occupational Annuity System**

Occupational annuities have enrolled over 45 million participants with a fund size of 1.5 trillion yuan, operating under an "8% employer contribution plus 4% employee contribution" model. In 2024, the investment return rate was 5.2%, with an average annual return of 5.29% over the past five years—significantly outperforming inflation. Compared to enterprise annuities, occupational annuities benefit from mandatory coverage and fiscal support. However, disparities persist between the pension benefits for government and public institution employees and those in the enterprise sector. As system integration deepens, the substitution effect of occupational annuities is gradually emerging, and policies such as tax incentives will be necessary to promote coordinated development with enterprise annuities.

③ **Differentiated Characteristics of the Supplementary Pension System**

Enterprise annuities face a "scale expansion but insufficient coverage" dilemma, whereas occupational annuities have achieved rapid growth driven by policy mandates, yet the two have not formed an effective linkage. In 2024, the combined coverage of enterprise and occupational annuities affected less than 100 million people—representing only 12% of the potential enrollee population—indicating that the supplementary protection function urgently needs strengthening. Future efforts should expand coverage through tax-deferred policies and enhance the quality of investment products, thereby transforming the second pillar from "partial coverage" to "comprehensive supplementation."

(3) **Exploration and Breakthroughs in the Third Pillar**

In 2024, the personal pension system was fully promoted nationwide, covering multiple products including insurance and funds. Exclusive commercial pension insurance features conservative accounts that guarantee interest rates of 2–3%, with aggressive account settlement rates reaching 4.25%. Pension target funds have reached a total scale of 94.7 billion yuan, with Y-class shares accounting for 9.3% of the market. However, the development faces three major challenges: first, product homogenization has resulted in 70% of products being conservative in nature; second, tax incentive strength is limited with an annual deduction cap of 12,000 yuan; third, and investor awareness is low, with only 38% of participants understanding the operation of the accounts. Future measures will need to optimize account design and diversify product offerings to help the third pillar become a significant force in market-oriented pension reserves.

(4) **Estimation and Analysis of the Sustainability of Pension Funds**
(1) **Explanation of the Estimation of the Basic Pension Gap for the First Pillar**

Based on the quasi-funded framework of China's urban employee basic pension insurance, this section constructs an actuarial model to estimate the pension fund gap. The estimation focuses on the first pillar, ignoring the rural and urban residents' pension insurance (which accounts for less than 20%) and conversion costs, and primarily analyzes the sustainability of the pooling account under the new system. The core assumptions include:

① **Financing Mechanism**: Employer contributions at 16% (for the pooling account under a pay-as-you-go system) + personal contributions at 8% (for the individual account under a funded system).
② **Demographic Parameters**: Based on the United Nations medium population projection, the proportion of the population aged 65 and above will exceed 20% by 2030 and reach 37.4% by 2060.
③ **Economic Parameters**: The average wage is assumed to grow at an annual real rate of 5%, and the replacement rate will gradually decline from 46% in 2020 to 40% and remain stable thereafter.
④ **Institutional Parameters**: The enrollment rate will increase from 50% in 2020 to 70% by 2060, while the retirement age will be gradually postponed from 2030 onward to 65 years.

(2) **Construction of the Revenue–Expenditure Model**

Following the estimation approach used by Song et al. (2015), the population distribution of a given year is employed to estimate the pension budget performance for that year. First, the total expenditure of the pension fund is calculated by dividing the population into five-year age cohorts. Assuming that the retirement age is 60, for age groups above retirement, it is assumed that the proportion of retirees participating in the pension scheme in that age group, the target replacement rate of pension benefits for that age group, and the average wage determine that year's total pension fund expenditure.

$$\begin{aligned} E_t = {} & P_{t,60\sim64}r_{t-5}q_{t-5}(0.6w_{t-5} + 0.4w_t) + P_{t,65\sim69}r_{t-10}q_{t-10}(0.6w_{t-10} + 0.4w_t) \\ & + P_{t,70\sim74}r_{t-15}q_{t-15}(0.6w_{t-15} + 0.4w_t) \\ & + P_{t,75\sim79}r_{t-20}q_{t-20}(0.6w_{t-20} + 0.4w_t) \\ & + P_{t,80}r_{t-25}q_{t-25}(0.6w_{t-25} + 0.4w_t) \end{aligned} \tag{2.1}$$

Equation (2.1) indicates that the expenditure for that year is the sum of pension benefits paid across the retirement age groups, where the pension benefits for each group are jointly determined by the wage received at retirement and the average wage of that year.

① **Income Model for Basic Pension Insurance of the First Pillar**

Similarly, the income of the pension fund is calculated. Assuming that the age of entry into the workforce is 20 years, that the pension contribution rate as a proportion of wages for that year is given, that the participation rate of the working-age population in the pension fund is provided, and that the average wage is known, then the total income of the pension fund for that year is expressed as follows:

$$I_t = P_{t,20-59} r_t \tau_t w_t \# \tag{2.2}$$

② **The Model for the Annual Surplus or Deficit of Pension Funds**

Based on Equations (2.2) and (2.3), assuming that the pension fund had a surplus or deficit of a certain amount in the previous year, the surplus or deficit for the current year is given by:

$$O_t = I_t - E_t + O_{t-1} \# \tag{2.3}$$

③ **The Model for the Cumulative Surplus or Cumulative Deficit of Pension Funds**

By the end of a given year, the cumulative surplus of the pension fund equals the cumulative surplus until that year plus the surplus of the current year, expressed as follows:

$$F_t = F_{t-1} + O_t \# \tag{2.4}$$

(3) **Parameter Assumptions and Key Data**

Indicator	2020	2030	2040	2050	2060
Elderly population (100 million)	1.91	2.6	3.5	4.8	5.7
Average wage (10,000 yuan)	7.9	20.74	45.45	99.5	217.6
Enrollment rate	50%	60%	65%	70%	70%
Replacement rate	46%	40%	40%	40%	40%

(4) **Estimation Results and Trend Analysis**

China's basic pension insurance fund faces medium- to long-term revenue–expenditure imbalances. From 2020 to 2035, the annual surplus will shift from 1.83 trillion yuan to a deficit of 1.49 trillion yuan, mainly due to the concentrated retirement of the baby boom cohort (born between 1962 and 1975), which will result in an average annual increase of 8 million new benefit recipients. After 2035, the deficit will expand at an accelerated pace, reaching 19.29 trillion yuan by 2060. This is attributable to the "scissors effect," driven by an annual growth rate of the elderly population at 2.5% coupled with a negative growth rate of the working-age population at –1.2%.

The cumulative surplus will peak at 8.68 trillion yuan in 2040 before rapidly depleted, with a historic inflection point of 3.16 trillion yuan occurring in 2050; by 2060, the cumulative deficit will exceed 21.88 trillion yuan, equivalent to 12.5% of GDP for that year (assuming a 5% average annual GDP growth rate). The sustainability of the system is thus facing severe challenges.

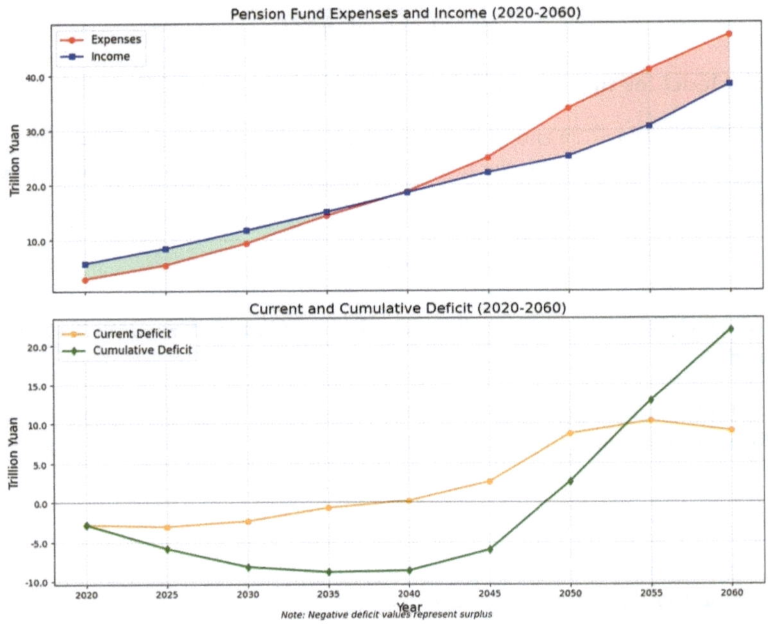

Further multi-scenario simulation analysis indicates that the policy instruments designed to address the long-term deficit within the basic pension system exhibit differentiated effects. The delayed retirement policy shows a strong leverage effect; each one-year extension of the retirement age can reduce the cumulative deficit by 3.2 trillion yuan in 2060 via both an extended contribution period (on average 3.2 years) and a compressed benefit-drawing period (on average 1.8 years). Adjustment of benefit levels is even more direct: a reduction in the replacement rate by 5 percentage points could reduce the deficit by 4.7 trillion yuan, which is equivalent to offsetting an increase in the dependency ratio of 2.6 percentage points. The policy effect of increasing the enrollment rate exhibits diminishing marginal benefits; a 10% increase in the enrollment rate may boost fund accumulation by 2.8 trillion yuan in the short term, but long-term gains are constrained by rigid demographic structures. It is noteworthy that wage growth acts as a "double-edged sword": an increase of 1% in the average wage growth rate will paradoxically widen the deficit by 1.5 trillion yuan. This is primarily due to the increase in the contribution base only yielding an income increase of approximately 0.8 trillion yuan, which fails to cover the expenditure expansion arising from the indexation of benefits (approximately 2.3 trillion yuan).

Simulation of policy combinations shows that if a two-year delay in retirement is implemented alongside a 3% reduction in the replacement rate, about 60% of the expected deficit can be eliminated while preserving the current purchasing power of benefits.

Policy variable	Impact on 2060 cumulative deficit for 1% change	Mechanism
Delayed retirement (1 year)	Reduction of 3.2 trillion yuan	Extends the contribution period while reducing the benefit-drawing period
Reduction in replacement rate (5%)	Reduction of 4.7 trillion yuan	Lowers benefit levels, thereby easing expenditure pressure
Increase in enrollment rate (10%)	Reduction of 2.8 trillion yuan	Expands the contribution base, enhancing the system's support ratio
Increase in wage growth (1%)	Increase of 1.5 trillion yuan	Raises the contribution base, yet benefit levels rise concur

Chapter 3
Reasons for Reforming the Pension System

3.1 China's Pension System Faces Significant Exogenous Pressures in the Medium to Long Term

3.1.1 Impact of the Economic Shock of Population Aging on Pension Equilibrium

The impact of population aging on the pension system is primarily manifested in the threefold challenge of shrinking labor supply, a declining contribution base, and rigidly growing pension expenditures. According to data from the National Bureau of Statistics, the proportion of people aged 65 and over in China surged from 9.7% in 2013 to 15.4% in 2023, and it is expected to exceed 37% by 2050, thus forming a "super-aged" society. This process affects the balance of pensions through the following mechanisms:

(1) **Shrinkage of Labor Supply and Decline in the Contribution Base**

Under a pay-as-you-go system, pension revenues depend on contributions made by the working-age population. However, between 2020 and 2070, China's working-age population (aged 15–64) is projected to decline sharply from 960 to 680 million, with an average annual decrease of 5.6 million—equivalent to the loss of the labor force of a mid-sized city every year. At the same time, labor-exporting provinces, such as Henan and Sichuan, will see their aging rates exceed 35%, while inflow regions like Guangdong will maintain aging rates below 25%, exacerbating regional disparities in contribution capabilities. Studies have shown that for every 1% increase in the dependency ratio, pension fund expenditures rise by approximately 658.02 basis points, whereas contribution revenues increase by only 0.72 percentage points, thereby accelerating the widening of the revenue–expenditure gap.

T. Wang et al., *China's Pension Reform*, Contributions to Finance and Accounting,
https://doi.org/10.1007/978-981-95-0103-8_3

(2) **Declining Savings Rate and Changes in Consumption Structure**

Population aging markedly reduces the household savings rate through the "life-cycle effect." Between 2010 and 2019, the household savings rate in China fell from 51.8% to 44.6%, while the proportion of rigid expenditures—such as on medical care and long-term care—increased from 11.3% to 17.5%. Older adults, as "net consumers," shift their consumption preferences from productive investments to service expenditures, leading to a slowdown in capital accumulation. OECD research indicates that due to aging, China's marginal return on capital has declined by 0.4–0.6% points, weakening the value appreciation potential of pension investments.

(3) **Intergenerational Imbalances in Human Capital Accumulation and Technological Progress**

Aging leads to an aging structure within research teams, with the proportion of researchers aged 60 and above rising from 21% in 2020 to 38% in 2070, while the share of young researchers declines to 19%, which dampens the momentum for technological innovation. Empirical studies show that for every 1 percentage point increase of aging, the growth rate of total factor productivity falls by 0.3 percentage points, thereby indirectly undermining the long-term returns of pension funds.

3.1.2 Impact of Population Aging on the Fiscal Burden of the Government

(1) **Rapid Increase in the Pressure for Pension Subsidies**

In 2023, fiscal subsidies for China's basic pension insurance funds accounted for 12.5% of fiscal expenditures, and this figure is expected to rise to 28.3% by 2070. Meanwhile, expenditures on science and technology may be compressed to 2.1% in the same period. When taking into account implicit debts (such as "empty" individual accounts), the actual fiscal burden becomes even more severe. Estimates indicate that, excluding fiscal subsidies, the urban employee basic pension fund will record its first deficit in 2028, with the cumulative gap possibly reaching 11.28 trillion yuan by 2050.

(2) **Exacerbation of Regional Fiscal Disparities**

Due to persistently low fertility rates (below 0.7) and ongoing population outflows, the three northeastern provinces are expected to enter a super-aged society by 2030, with the pension gap reaching 12.5% of GDP—approaching levels observed during the Greek debt crisis. In contrast, border regions such as Tibet and Xinjiang will maintain aging rates below 15%, necessitating that central fiscal transfers via inter-provincial adjustment funds balance the regional burden. By 2022, the adjustment ratio had already reached 20%.

(3) **Intergenerational Equity and Fiscal Sustainability Conflicts**

Under the current system, the concentrated retirement of the baby boom generation (born between 1962 and 1975) will add an average of 8 million new retirees each year, but their individual account accumulations are insufficient and heavily rely on fiscal transfer payments. Estimates suggest that if no reforms are undertaken, the basic pension replacement rate will fall below 30% by 2048—far below the international warning line of 55%.

3.1.3 Impact of Inadequate Household Retirement Savings on the Sustainability of the Pension System

(1) **Imbalances in Household Savings Structure**

In Chinese households, nearly 80% of assets are allocated to real estate, while bank deposits account for more than 50% of financial assets, and pension reserves constitute merely 1.2%. By 2025, the pension savings gap for middle-income families is projected to reach 1.4 million yuan, which must cover the effects of inflation (an average of 3.5% per year), rising medical costs (growing at 6.5% per year), and long-term care expenses (amounting to 0.8–1.2% of GDP).

(2) **Lag in the Development of the Third Pillar**

As of 2024, the contribution rate to personal pension accounts is less than 5%, with an average annual contribution of only 3,200 yuan—far below the upper limit of 12,000 yuan. A key issue is the insufficient tax incentives: under the EET system, high-income groups effectively receive only a 4.8% tax benefit, while middle- and low-income groups, due to their lower marginal tax rates, have weak incentives to participate. By comparison, the asset size of Chinese personal pension accounts is only 1/50th of that of American IRA accounts.

(3) **Transmission of Intergenerational Transfer Pressures**

The weakening of the family's role in providing elderly support exacerbates dependence on public pensions. In 2023, the average monthly basic pension for rural and urban residents was only 240 yuan, which is equivalent to merely 12% of the per capita disposable income in rural areas; this forces families to compensate via "cross-generational caregiving" and "real estate exchanges." However, with the low liquidity of real estate, a decline in the demand for "passing the baton" after 2025 could trigger asset depreciation.

3.1.4 Simulation

Considering the systemic and global impact of population aging on the economy—which affects pension system parameters through multiple channels such as economic growth, household wealth accumulation, and fiscal stability—a purely endogenous analysis of pension sustainability is likely to underestimate future benefit pressures. Therefore, this paper constructs a multi-sector dynamic stochastic general equilibrium (DSGE) model. In this model, the household sector is divided into working households and retired households, and two types of structural pension equations are incorporated, representing a government-led and an individual-led pension model, to simulate the differential effects of fee reduction policies under different pension regimes. The model's principal contribution lies in introducing households' expectations regarding aging, thereby capturing the decision-making adjustments of the household sector as the social pension burden deepens. Traditional fiscal and monetary policies, such as fee reduction policies and government investment, are also incorporated. By solving the model and employing Bayesian estimation based on empirical Chinese data, the analysis focuses on the impacts arising from evolving preferences and adjustments in pension models in the context of an aging society.

① **Household Sector**

To examine the effects of different pension models and pension expectations individually, the paper specifies two pension models and two types of household agents. Under the government-coordinated pension model, it is assumed that future pension expenses for working households are borne by the government under a pay-as-you-go system, and that post-retirement consumption depends solely on the pension income received at that time. In contrast, under the household-coordinated pension model, working households undergo pension planning within an accumulation-based system, causing their current consumption expenditures to reflect intertemporal balance. Regarding household agents, working households are modeled as the standard household sector in the economic model, whereas retired households are assumed to be excluded from the labor market—thus unable to earn wage income through labor—but they receive retirement pension income at a predetermined standard. After describing the behavior of each type of economic agent, the model addresses the aggregation of these behaviors to yield the overall behavior of the economy.

(A) **Government-Coordinated Pension Model (Two-Agent Framework)**

Unlike the overlapping generations (OLG) framework—where households plan for their own retirement—the government-coordinated pension model (Two-Agent Framework) assumes that individuals make no personal retirement plans, and that the government entirely assumes the pension responsibility. It is assumed that there exists a continuum of consumers, denoted by an index $h \in [0, 1]$. A segment of the population consists of working households that are active in the labor market ϕ, making decisions regarding labor supply and renting their labor to firms; these agents are indicated by a specific subscript $i \in [0, \phi]$. The remainder comprises retired households, who, being restricted from labor supply decisions, invest in physical capital; they are denoted by another subscript $i \in [\phi, 1]$.

(a) **Working Households**

The utility function for working households is given by:

$$E_t \sum_{k=0}^{\infty} \beta^k \left[\frac{C_{w,t+k}^{1-\sigma}}{1-\sigma} - \chi \frac{N_{w,t+k}^{1+\eta}}{1+\eta} \right] \tag{3.1}$$

where $C_{w,t}$ denotes private consumption, β is the discount factor reflects the subjective discount rate, χ is another parameter represents the weight on labor supply, σ is the coefficient of relative risk aversion is specified, η is the reciprocal of the labor supply elasticity is included, and a term to represent a one-time lump-sum tax is T_t. The budget constraint faced by households is formalized as:

$$C_{w,t} + I_{w,t} + T_t = (1 - \tau_t^w) \frac{W_t}{P_t} N_{w,t} + \frac{R_t^k}{P_t} K_{w,t-1} \tag{3.2}$$

The capital accumulation constraint is given by:

$$C_{w,t} + I_{w,t} + T_t = (1 - \tau_t^w) \frac{W_t}{P_t} N_{w,t} + \frac{R_t^k}{P_t} K_{w,t-1} \tag{3.3}$$

If this equation is incorporated simultaneously with the retired household's equation, collinearity may occur.

$$C_{w,t} + K_{w,t} - K_{w,t-1}(1 - \delta) = \left(1 - \tau_t^w\right) w_t N_{w,t} + r_t^k K_{w,t-1} \tag{3.4}$$

In this framework, household income derives from after-tax wage income, capital gains, and bond interest income, while expenditures primarily cover consumption, investment, and the purchase of government bonds, as well as a one-time lump-sum tax remitted to the government—this tax represents both the labor tax rate and the personal pension insurance contribution.

(b) **Retired Households**

It is assumed that retired households no longer participate in the labor market. Their utility function is given by:

$$E_t \sum_{k=0}^{\infty} (\beta_r)^k \left[\frac{C_{r,t+k}^{1-\sigma}}{1-\sigma} \right] \tag{3.5}$$

Retired households allocate all their income to consumption and bond purchases, where income is obtained from government-payout pensions and bond interest. Their budget constraints are formulated as:

$$C_{r,t} + I_{r,t} = S_t + \frac{R_t^k}{P_t} K_{r,t-1} \tag{3.6}$$

$$K_{r,t} - K_{r,t-1}(1 - \delta) - I_{r,t} = 0 \tag{3.7}$$

$$C_{r,t} + K_{r,t} - K_{r,t-1}(1 - \delta) = S_t + r_t^k K_{r,t-1} \tag{3.8}$$

(c) **Aggregation of the Household Sector Under the Government-Coordinated Pension Model**

The aggregate value of each variable in the household sector is given by:

$$X_t = \int_0^1 X_{h,t} d(h) = \phi X_{w,t} + (1 - \phi) X_{r,t} \tag{3.9}$$

$$C_t = \phi C_{w,t} + (1 - \phi) C_{r,t} \tag{3.10}$$

$$K_t = \phi K_{w,t} + (1 - \phi) K_{r,t} \tag{3.11}$$

$$I_t = \phi I_{w,t} + (1 - \phi) I_{r,t} \tag{3.12}$$

$$N_t = \phi N_{w,t} \tag{3.13}$$

$$K_t - K_{t-1}(1 - \delta) - I_t = 0 \tag{3.14}$$

(B) **Household-Coordinated Pension Model (OLG Framework)**

Diamond (1965) incorporated the life cycle into the microfoundations of household decision making, forming the overlapping generations (OLG) model. The key difference between this and the government-coordinated (Two-Agent) model is that households consider their own retirement conditions when maximizing intertemporal utility. Following the DSGE-OLG model set out by Baksa and Munkacsi (2016), it is assumed that there exists a representative household whose working consumption and retirement consumption jointly determine its intertemporal substitution elasticity:

$$\underset{C_{w,t},N_{w,t},C_{r,t}}{MAX} : U_t = E_t \left(\sum_{i=0}^{\infty} \beta^i \left[\begin{array}{c} \left(1 - \omega_{w,t}\right)^i \left[\dfrac{C_{w,t+i}^{1-\sigma}}{1 - \sigma} - \chi \dfrac{N_{w,t+i}^{1+\eta}}{1 + \eta} \right] + \\ \left(1 - \omega_{w,t}\right)^{i-1} \left(\omega_{w,t}\right) \left[\dfrac{C_{r,t+i}^{1-\sigma}}{1 - \sigma} \right] \end{array} \right] \right) \tag{3.15}$$

Assume that new workers continuously enter the workforce, forming working households, while retired households consume their entire income before exiting. The number of entrants equals the number of exits. In period t, the budget constraint for working households (based on actual inflows and outflows) is as follows:

(a) **If Not Retired (with Probability [·]):**

$$C_{w,t} + I_{w,t} + I_{r,t} + T_t = (1 - \tau_t^w)\frac{W_t}{P_t}N_{w,t} + \frac{R_t^k}{P_t}K_{w,t-1} \tag{3.16}$$

In the absence of retirement, household income is derived from wages and capital income, which is allocated between consumption and investment. At this stage, investment can be directed toward either the capital stock maintained by the working household or saved as retirement capital stock for the retired household. A one-time lump-sum tax is also imposed.

(b) **If Retired (with Probability [·]):**

$$C_{r,t} = \frac{R_t^k}{P_t}K_{r,t-1} + S_t \tag{3.17}$$

After retirement, households consume their entire wealth (including pensions), with capital accumulation following the technology:

$$C_{r,t} = \frac{R_t^k}{P_t}K_{r,t-1} + S_t \tag{3.18}$$

$$K_{r,t} = K_{r,t-1}(1 - \delta) + I_{r,t} \tag{3.19}$$

② **Firm Sector**

It is assumed that intermediate goods firms operate in a monopolistically competitive market with a production function of the C-D form:

$$Y_t = Z_t(K_{t-1})^{\alpha}(N_t)^{1-\alpha} \tag{3.20}$$

$$log(Z_t) = \rho_z log(Z_{t-1}) + \epsilon_t^z, \ \epsilon_t^z \sim (0, \sigma_z^2) \tag{3.21}$$

Here, [·] represents total factor productivity, which is assumed to follow an AR (1) process. Given that China's basic pension insurance system combines social pooling with individual accounts—where employer and individual contributions are the major sources of fund revenue—the pension insurance fee collection behavior is incorporated into the optimization process of intermediate goods firms. Following Coenen et al. (2012), it is assumed that firms pay pension insurance fees at a wage-based rate, and that by subjecting this rate to shocks, phased reductions in employer pension insurance contributions can be simulated. For intermediate goods firms, the cost-minimization problem is expressed as:

$$MIN : (1 + \tau_t^{fs})W_t N_t + R_t^k K_t \tag{3.22}$$

$$P_t Z_t (K_{t-1})^{\alpha} (N_t)^{1-\alpha} \geq P_t Y_t \tag{3.23}$$

Solving yields the wage rate and the return on capital for a given firm j:

$$\frac{\left(1 + \tau_t^{fs}\right) W_t}{P_t} = (1 - \alpha) Z_t \left(\frac{K_{t-1}}{N_t}\right)^{\alpha} = (1 - \alpha)\left(\frac{Y_t}{N_t}\right) \tag{3.24}$$

$$\frac{R_t^k}{P_t} = \alpha Z_t \left(\frac{K_{t-1}}{N_t}\right)^{\alpha - 1} = \alpha \left(\frac{Y_t}{K_{t-1}}\right) \tag{3.25}$$

which leads to their ratio:

$$\frac{\left(1 + \tau_t^{fs}\right) W_t}{R_t^k} = \frac{1 - \alpha}{\alpha} \frac{K_t}{N_t} \tag{3.26}$$

After eliminating price effects and converting to real wages and real returns on capital, one obtains:

$$\frac{\left(1 + \tau_t^{fs}\right) w_t}{r_t^K} = \frac{1 - \alpha}{\alpha} \frac{K_t}{N_t} \tag{3.27}$$

③ **Social Security Sector**

According to the Social Insurance Law, China's basic pension insurance operates by combining social pooling with individual accounts. The pension fund is composed of contributions from employers and employees, as well as government subsidies. Additionally, the social insurance fund is invested in accordance with State Council regulations to preserve and increase its value, while ensuring safety. It is assumed that the social security department disburses pensions in proportion to the number of retirees, while investing the remaining portion in government bonds to earn interest income in the subsequent year. Hence, social security income comprises employer contributions (based on the wage levels of working households), individual contributions, and government subsidies, where [·] denotes the government bond interest rate. Social security expenditures include both the proportion retained for social security investments and the pension disbursements. Specifically:

$$R_t^{social} = \left(\tau_t^{fs} + \tau_t^{w}\right) W_t N_{w,t} + P_t G_t^{Social} \tag{3.28}$$

$$E_t^{social} = P_t S_t \tag{3.29}$$

The specific budget balance is set as follows:

$$\left(\tau_t^{fs} + \tau_t^{age}\right) w_t N_t + G_t^{Social} = S_t \tag{3.30}$$

Assuming government fiscal balance is maintained by:

$$\mathcal{G}_t^{Social} = T_t. \tag{3.31}$$

Pension disbursements are linked to the wage income of working households and are paid out proportionally (according to the replacement rate):

$$\mathcal{S}_t = \phi^s N_{w,t} w_t \tag{3.32}$$

Note: Here, social security disbursements must exceed employee contributions, i.e., $S_t > \tau N_{w,t}, W_t$. Under this setup, if S_t is given, then the government's fiscal gap $G_t \equiv S_t - \tau N_{w,t}, W_t$ is also determined, implying that the government fully covers the gap.

(2) **Parameter Calibration**

See Table 3.1.

(3) **Simulation Analysis**

① **Analysis of the Impact of Accelerated Population Aging on the Balance of Pension Revenues and Expenditures**

Based on the equilibrium solution of a three-period OLG model and parameter calibration, with a labor force growth rate is γ_L = −0.8%, a basic pension contribution rate is θ_p = 28%, and a pension replacement rate is τ = 60%. Figure 3.1

Table 3.1 Parameter calibration table

Parameter name	Calibrated value	Parameter name	Calibrated value
Capital marginal productivity elasticity	0.33	Depreciation rate	0.025
Relative risk aversion coefficient	2	Pension replacement rate	0.6
Discount factor (subjective discount rate)	0.97	Enterprise pension contribution rate	0.16
Labor supply weight parameter	1	Labor tax rate	0.08
Inverse of labor supply elasticity	1.5	Retirement probability in household-integrated pension model	0.2

illustrates the impulse response of the pension system to a sudden 1.5% point increase in the elderly dependency ratio.

Numerical simulation results indicate that demographic shocks will trigger a sustained widening of the pension revenue–expenditure gap, with the dynamic transmission exhibiting marked asymmetry. When the shock to the elderly dependency ratio occurs, pension revenues immediately drop by 0.38% points, while on the expenditure side, due to the stickiness in benefit adjustments, the increase is only 0.12 percentage points. Over time, the multiplier effects of a shrinking contributor base and a growing beneficiary population begin to materialize: by the fifth period, cumulative revenues have declined by 2.1 percentage points while expenditures, driven by the mechanism of indexation for retirees, have cumulatively risen by 3.7 percentage points, causing the fund gap to breach a warning threshold of 2.6 percentage points. This dynamic path reveals a dual rigidity in the institutional design: a contribution base constrained by the elasticity of labor supply, which is slow to adjust, and benefit expenditures that display institutional inertial delays due to political decision lags.

By comparing simulation scenarios with different policy parameters (Fig. 3.2), it is found that under a delayed retirement policy scenario (with the retirement age postponed by 0.3 years annually), the peak gap can be reduced by 41.2%, although policy time lags cause the gap to expand 12.7% more rapidly in the first 10 periods. When an automatic balancing mechanism is introduced—adjusting the contribution rate and replacement rate based on the elasticity with respect to the dependency ratio—the mid-term balance improves significantly, with the cumulative gap by period 20 reduced by 58.3%. The heterogeneity of these policy effects originates from the threefold transmission mechanism of demographic shocks:

(A) **Labor Supply Channel:** A 1% reduction in the working-age population directly causes pension fund revenues to decline by 0.68% through a contraction in the contribution base ($\alpha = 0.68$).
(B) **Intergenerational Transfer Channel:** A 1% increase in the share of the elderly causes pension expenditures to rise by 0.92% due to rigid increases in benefits ($\beta = 0.92$).
(C) **Fiscal Feedback Channel:** For every 1% expansion in the gap, the pressure on government fiscal subsidies increases by 0.33% ($\gamma = 0.33$), thereby reinforcing a cycle of deficit accumulation.

Sensitivity tests (see Table 3.3) indicate that when improvements in human capital quality is taken into account (with labor productivity growing at an average of 1.2% per year), the speed of mid-term gap expansion slows by 28.4%; however, if low fertility persists (with the total fertility rate ≤ 1.3), the cumulative fund gap by 2050 will exceed 3.2% of GDP. These findings corroborate the conclusions reached by Feng Jin (2019) regarding the compensatory effects of population quality dividends, and they also reveal the profound impact of the low-fertility trap on the social security system, as highlighted by Wang Wei (2021).

② Analysis of the Dynamic Response of Pension Pressure to Insufficient Household Retirement Reserves

Within an overlapping generations (OLG) framework, Fig. 3.1 shows the dynamic response path of the key pension system variables when the level of household retirement reserves decreases by 10%. The Numerical simulation results indicate that insufficient household retirement reserves elevate pension pressure through a dual transmission mechanism: firstly, a 1% point reduction in the household saving rate directly increases the dependency of retirees on public pensions by 0.8 percentage points; secondly, every 5 percentage point decline in the pension insurance replacement rate forces the social security department to expand the scale of pension disbursements by 2.3%. The economic transmission path of these parameter changes operates as follows: when household pension account accumulation is inadequate, precautionary saving motives in the early periods prompt the working-age population to reduce current consumption (by an amount equivalent to 0.6% of GDP); however, due to liquidity constraints, this adjustment cannot fully offset the shortfall in retirement reserves, and the pressure ultimately transfers to the public pension system.

More in-depth scenario simulations show that when the elasticity coefficient of intergenerational transfer payments is set to 0.15, the crowding-out effect of insufficient household retirement reserves on public pensions is significantly amplified. Specifically, the annual growth rate of pension expenditure pressure increases from 1.2% in the baseline scenario to 1.8%, with the revenue–expenditure gap expanding by 1.5 times the baseline value. The transmission mechanism underlying this outcome is that when a household's capacity for intergenerational support is weaker, retirees become more dependent on institutional pension protection, causing the impact of insufficient household reserves on the public system to be nonlinearly amplified.

These simulation results are strongly corroborated by recent empirical evidence, such as the downward trend in household saving rates revealed by the Seventh National Census (National Bureau of Statistics, 2021) and the fact that the growth rate of pension fund expenditures has consistently outpaced that of revenues (Ministry of Human Resources and Social Security, 2023).

③ Impact Identification Analysis of Government Debt Resolution on Pensions

Based on an overlapping generations framework within a dynamic stochastic general equilibrium (DSGE) model, Fig. 3.2 illustrates the shock transmission path of key variables in the pension system when the scale of government debt resolution reaches 2% of GDP. Numerical simulations indicate that for each 0.1 unit increase in the fiscal adjustment coefficient θ, the current pension gap expands by 0.8 percentage points, and there is a significant intertemporal transmission effect—such that over five years, the cumulative gap can expand up to 2.3 times the initial shock. This nonlinear transmission mechanism is manifested by the fact that for every 1 yuan reduction in government fiscal expenditures, only 0.45 yuan can be recouped via the social security contribution compensation channel, leaving the residual gap to force a 1.2% reduction in the pension replacement rate, which in turn induces the intertemporal consumption substitution elasticity of households to rise to 1.8.

More detailed scenario simulations indicate that under a baseline scenario of 0.3 and a strengthened adjustment scenario of 0.5, when the intensity of fiscal adjustment is raised to 3% of GDP, the intergenerational transfer payment mechanism undergoes a structural change. Specifically, the precautionary saving rate of the working-age population will increase sharply by 4.2 percentage points; however, constrained by the law of diminishing marginal propensity to consume, this adjustment can only offset 42% of the losses in pension revenues. This ratchet effect of fiscal adjustment is especially pronounced in sensitivity tests: if the duration of fiscal adjustment exceeds five years, the cumulative pension gap will surpass 1.5% of GDP and trigger a concave loss in the social welfare function.

These simulation results are highly consistent with empirical evidence, such as the fiscal adjustment–social security compensation elasticity of 0.32 revealed in the Ministry of Finance's local government bond stress test report (2024) and household consumption surveys indicating that every 1% decline in the pension replacement rate is associated with a 0.7% increase in the saving rate (National Development and Reform Commission, 2023). This confirms that there is a significant amplification effect on the fragility of the pension system during government debt resolution—particularly when the intensity of fiscal adjustment exceeds the threshold, which may trigger a precipitous decline in overall social welfare levels.

3.2 Analysis of the Limitations of Parameter Reforms

3.2.1 Current Status of Parameter Reforms

(1) **Fee Parameter Adjustment System**

① **Gradual Delayed Retirement Policy**

China is mitigating the pressures of population aging by implementing a phased delay in retirement. Starting in 2025, female retirement ages will be postponed by 4 months per year and male retirement ages by 2 months per year, with the ultimate goal of unifying the retirement age at 65 for both genders by 2045. This policy extends the labor supply period and expand the contribution base. Actuarial analyses indicate that it can delay pension fund deficits for urban employees by 5–8 years (Li Hanwei, 2023). The policy permits flexible retirement choices, allowing employees to retire early or late (up to 3 years) based on the minimum contribution years, thereby balancing individual rights with the sustainability of the system.

② **Normalization Reform of the Contribution Base**

Reforms enacted in 2019 expanded the statistical scope of the average wage to a comprehensive measure (including private enterprises) and gradually increased the lower limit of the contribution base to 80% of the comprehensive wage benchmark (targeted for 2025). For example, in Zhejiang, the lower limit of the contribution base in 2024 is determined 60% of the comprehensive average wage, amounting to 4,812 yuan per month—an increase of 350 yuan from the previous year. Although the nominal contribution rate for flexible employment has been reduced to 16%, the expansion of the base has led to a 13.6% rise in actual contributions (Sun Qixiang, 2021), thereby enhancing the stability of fund revenues. Nationwide, regions such as Beijing adjusted the upper and lower limits of the contribution base in 2023, reflecting the standardization effect of comprehensive wage statistics.

③ **Mechanism for Extending the Minimum Contribution Duration**

To address longevity risk, the minimum contribution period will increase by one year every five years from 2025, reaching 25 years by 2040. Research by Zheng Bingwen (2022) indicates that each additional year of contribution improves the long-term balance ratio of the fund by 0.8 percentage points. If employees contribute for 25 years starting at age 25, the pension replacement rate may increase by approximately 10 percentage points, thereby reducing reliance on the pooling fund after retirement.

(2) **Benefit Parameter Adjustment Mechanism**

① **Dynamic Adjustment of the Pension Accrual Coefficient**

A regulatory factor, α, which is linked to the system's dependency ratio (α = √(dependency ratio /baseline dependency ratio)), is introduced into the calculation of the basic pension. Adjustments are triggered when the dependency ratio exceeds 2.8. According to Wang Xiaojun's (2023) model, if the dependency ratio declines from 2.8 to 1.5, the α value falls from 1 to 0.73, thereby correspondingly reducing the basic pension coefficient and alleviating expenditure pressures.

② **Differentiated Adjustment of Benefit Growth Rates**

A "dual-linkage" mechanism is established: 60% of the growth rate is pegged to the CPI to safeguard purchasing power, while 40% is linked to the average wage to share the benefits of growth. When the number of months that the fund surplus can cover falls below 9, a reduction coefficient ranging from 0.5 to 0.8 is activated. For instance, in 2022 in a certain province, when the fund could cover payments for 8 months, the pension growth rate was reduced from 5 to 4%. In 2024, the nationwide adjustment ratio was uniformly set at 3%, employing a combination of fixed adjustment (with per capita adjustments of 40–45 yuan), linkage adjustments (with both contribution years and pension levels tied to the growth rate), and preferential adjustments (for seniors and residents in arduous areas), to balance fairness with incentive.

③ **Urban-Rural Residents' Pension Adjustment Mechanism**

A benefit determination and basic pension regular adjustment mechanism was established in 2018. In 2024, the national minimum basic pension standard was raised by 20 yuan to 145–185 yuan/month (e.g., Jilin and Xinjiang), representing a 19.4% increase. Local governments may additionally provide supplementary seniority-based and longevity-based basic pensions for those aged 65 and above and long-term contributors, strengthening the principle of "more contributions, more benefits; longer contributions, more benefits."

(3) **Optimization of Fiscal Subsidy Parameters**

① **Central Adjustment Fund Multiplier Model**

In 2023, the adjustment ratio was increased to 4.5%. Regional balance is achieved by applying the formulas "Upper Adjustment Limit = Number of Insured Persons × Unit Rate × Average Wage × Adjustment Ratio" and "Adjustment Coefficient = MAX (0, 1 – (Province's Reserve Months/National Average Reserve Months))". In 2022, the scale of the adjustment fund reached 930 billion yuan, effectively alleviating payment pressures in regions such as Northeast China.

② **Dynamic Equilibrium of State-Owned Capital Transfers**

Three batches of central enterprise equity transfers, totaling 1.68 trillion yuan, have been completed. When the fund's reserve months are less than 3 months, the dividend payout proportion is increased to 30%. In 2023, following the triggering of this mechanism in a certain province, additional proceeds of 20 billion yuan were obtained, accounting for 5% of the fund revenue, thereby achieving a sustainable "asset-based support for old-age" path.

(4) Key Achievements

Through the tri-dimensional linkage of "expanding the base, curbing outflows, and providing a safety net", China's parameter reforms for pensions have significantly enhanced system resilience. On the contribution side, the gradual delayed retirement policy has postponed deficits in urban employee pension funds by 5–8 years; in 2023, delayed retirement increased the number of contributors by 15 million, raising revenues by approximately 48 billion yuan. The comprehensive average wage reform has expanded the contribution base, with the actual contributions from flexible employees rising by 13.6%, leading to an 8.7% increase in fund revenues in regions such as Zhejiang in 2024. On the benefits side, the dynamic adjustment mechanism linking the basic pension to the dependency ratio enabled one province to save 5 billion yuan in expenditures in 2024; the "dual-linkage" mechanism for enhancing benefit growth preserved purchasing power, with a 3% nationwide pension adjustment in 2024 and a 19.4% increase in the minimum standard for urban and rural residents' pensions. On the fiscal side, the central adjustment fund reached 930 billion yuan in 2022, with reserve months in Heilongjiang increasing from 2 to 5; state-owned capital transfers totaling 1.68 trillion yuan enabled a province to secure an additional 20 billion yuan in dividends in 2023.

(5) Existing Issues

The reform faces multiple challenges. On the contribution side, the pace of delayed retirement is faster for women than for men, which raises questions about fairness; moreover, the contribution burden index for flexible workers has reached 28%, prompting some low-income groups to exit the system. On the benefit side, the transparency of the dynamic adjustment of the pension accrual coefficient is insufficient. In 2023, an adjustment triggered by a decline in the dependency ratio in one province led to criticisms from retirees, and in some regions, the growth rate in benefits falls below the rate of CPI inflation. On the fiscal side, the effectiveness of the central adjustment fund relies on administrative interventions and suffers from a lack of market-oriented operational mechanisms, while mandatory dividends from state-owned capital might affect long-term corporate investments. Additionally, significant regional disparities exist in fiscal subsidy capacity; for example, pension subsidies for urban and rural residents in Shanghai reach 730 yuan per year, whereas in Tibet they amount to only 100 yuan per year, exacerbating benefit inequality. In the future, it will be necessary to enhance policy flexibility, optimize the contribution structure, improve transparency, and strengthen market mechanisms in a coordinated effort to promote the development of a multi-pillar system and achieve sustainable institutional development.

3.2.2 *Simulation*

(1) **Model Construction**

To examine the impact of population aging on the economic system and the subsequent changes in the sustainability of the pension system, this study constructs a computable general equilibrium (CGE) model encompassing 42 industries. The model's economic modules primarily include production and trade, economic agents, pensions, market equilibrium, and macroeconomic closure. Based on this analytical framework, the paper further conducts comparative simulation analyses of various pension reform proposals.

① Aggregate Output

Assume that the aggregate production function takes a CES form; the output of each sector comprises two components—intermediate inputs and value-added inputs—while the value of the product is the sum of the values of intermediate and value-added inputs. This relationship is derived from the cost-minimization condition:

$$QA_a = a_a^q\left[\delta_a^q QVA_a^{\rho_a} + \left(1 - \delta_a^q\right)QINTA_a^{\rho_a}\right]^{\frac{1}{\rho_a}}$$

$$PA_a \cdot QA_a = PVA_a \cdot QVA_a + PINTA_a \cdot QINTA_a$$

$$\frac{PVA_a}{PINTA_a} = \frac{\delta_a^q}{1 - \delta_a^q}\left(\frac{QINTA_a}{QVA_a}\right)^{1-\rho_a} \quad a \in A$$

where δ_a^q represents the elasticity of substitution in output, ρ_a^q is the output from value-added inputs, and α_a^q denotes total factor productivity.

② Value-Added Component

Assume that the value-added component is produced jointly by labor and capital in a CES functional form. The government imposes separate taxes on labor and capital at rates of tval and tavk, respectively. Thus, the value-added component consists of three parts: the value of labor, the value of capital, and the value-added tax. From the optimality conditions, one obtains:

$$QVA_a = a_a^{va}[\delta_a^{va} QLD_a^{\rho_a^{va}} + (1 - \delta_a^{va}) QKD_a^{\rho_a^{va}}]^{\frac{1}{\rho_a^{va}}}$$

$$PVA_a \cdot QVA_a = (1 + tavl) \cdot WL \cdot QLD_a + (1 + tavk) \cdot WK \cdot QLK_a$$

$$\frac{WL \cdot (1 + tval)}{WK \cdot (1 + tvak)} = \frac{\delta_a^{va}}{1 - \delta_a^{va}} \left(\frac{QKD_a}{QLD_a} \right)^{1-\rho_a^{va}} \quad a \in A$$

where WL is the price of labor, WK the price of capital, ρ_a^{va} the elasticity of substitution between factors, δ_a^{va} the output share of labor, and α_a^{va} the parameter for total factor productivity.

③ Intermediate Input Component

Assume that intermediate inputs are of the Leontief type. In an open economy, intermediate inputs $QINTA_{ca}$ are priced at $PINTA_{ca}$, and they form the domestic supply of goods, which is the sum of domestic production and imports. The output of each sector, corresponding to a given good, is the product of the quantity of intermediate inputs and the input–output coefficient. Similarly, the price composition of intermediate inputs is determined by:

$$QINTA_{ca} = ica_{ca} \cdot QINTA_a \quad a \in A, c \in C$$

$$PINTA_{ca} = \sum\nolimits_{c \in C} ica_{ca} \cdot PQ_c a \in A$$

Domestic production of goods comprises both domestic sales and exports, with the price of domestically produced and sold goods denoted by PDA_a andsssssss the price of exported goods by PE_a

$$QA_a = \alpha_a^l \left[\delta_a^l QDA_a^{\rho_a^l} + \left(1 - \delta_a^l\right) QE_a^{\rho_a^l} \right]^{\frac{1}{\rho_a^l}} \rho_a^l > 1, a \in A$$

$$\frac{PDA_a}{PE_a} = \frac{\delta^l}{1 - \delta_a^l} \left(\frac{QE_a}{QDA_a} \right)^{1-\rho_a^l}, a \in A$$

$$PA_a = PDA_a \cdot \frac{QDA_a}{QA_a} + PE_a \cdot \frac{QE_a}{QA_a}, a \in A$$

Export prices are jointly determined by international market prices and the exchange rate:

$$PE_a = pwe_a(1 - te_a) \cdot EXR, a \in A$$

where EXR denotes the exchange rate, pwe_a represents the duty-paid offshore value of the good measured in foreign currency, and te_a is the export tax.

The quantity of goods supplied in the domestic market meets the final demand of domestic agents (including consumers, enterprises, and the government) as well as the intermediate input requirements for production. This supply is assumed to consist of domestically produced and sold goods and imported goods, with their substitution relationship described by the Armington condition. Likewise, the optimality conditions yield:

$$\mathcal{QQ}_c = \alpha_c^q \left(\delta_c^q \mathcal{QDC}_c^{\rho_c^q} + (1 - \delta_c^q) \mathcal{QM}_c^{\rho_c^q} \right)^{\frac{1}{\rho_c^q}}, c \in \mathcal{C}$$

$$\frac{PDC_c}{PM_c} = \frac{\delta_c^q}{1 - \delta_c^q} \left(\frac{QM_c}{QDC_c} \right)^{1-\rho_c^q}, c \in C$$

$$PQ_c = PDC_c \cdot \frac{QDC_c}{QQ_c} + PM_c \frac{QM_c}{QQ_c}, c \in C$$

$$PM_c = pwm_c(1 + tm_c) EXR_{,c} \in C$$

Within the domestic market, the price of domestically produced and sold goods is given by PDC_c, the price of imported goods by PM_c, tm_c denotes the import tariff, and pwm is the price of goods measured in foreign currency.

Since domestically produced and sold goods correspond one-to-one with production activities, it follows that:

④ Household Sector

To examine the mechanisms by which population aging influences pensions, the model assumes that the economy contains two types of residents:the young and the elderly. The young generate income from labor, capital income, and deferred tax savings arising from the purchase of personal pensions. Their expenditures include consumption, investment, income taxes, and pension contributions. In contrast, the elderly receive income from returns on capital, accumulations in personal pension accounts, pension disbursements from the pooling account, and after-tax deferred personal pension income. The incomes of the young and the elderly are given by:

$$YH^y = (1 - ti_h - \theta_1) WL \cdot QLS + ti_{pp} SH_{pp}^o + \theta_2 WK \cdot QLK$$

$$YH^o = (1 - \theta_2) shift_{h,k} WK \cdot QLK + transfr_{h,gov} y_h + SH_s^o + (1 - ti_{pp}) SH_{pp}^o$$

where 0 c

θ_1 denotes the proportion of pension contributions paid by the young; ti_h represents the tax on personal labor income; ti_k corresponds to the tax on capital income; $shif_{hk}$ is the share of capital income distributed to households; θ_2 is the allocation ratio of capital income between the young and the elderly; $transfr_{h,gov}$ denotes the proportion of government transfer payments from the pooling account to the elderly; and y_h is the average wage level. For simplicity, the model assumes that household savings exist entirely in the form of accumulated deposits in personal pension accounts, with SH_s^0 representing the accumulated deferred personal pension income and SH_{pp}^0 the deferred tax rate. Consequently, household disposable income and consumption demand are given by:

$$PQ_c \cdot QH_c = \delta^{ODR} \cdot shrh_c^y \cdot mpc^y \cdot YH^y + (1 - \delta^{ODR}) \cdot shrh_c^o \cdot mpc^o \cdot YH^o$$

where δ^{ODR} denotes 1/(1 + Elderly Dependency Ratio), mpc the marginal propensity to consume of the group, and $shrh_c$ the consumption share for the group.

$$SH^y = YH^y - \sum_c \delta^{ODR} \cdot shrh_c^y \cdot mpc^y \cdot YH^y - I^y = SH_s^y + SH_{pp}^y$$

SH^y represents the savings of the young, defined as the gap between current income and the sum of consumption and investment expenditures, including contributions to personal pension accounts and purchases of deferred personal pensions.

⑤ Firms

A firm's pre-tax income is the return on its capital inputs, where [blank] is the share of capital income allocated to the firm, $shif_{pp,k}$] is the share associated with deferred personal pensions, and the distribution is given by $shif_{ent,k}$+$shif_{h,k}$+$shif_{pp,k}$. Firm savings are balanced with post-tax income, where ti_{ent} represents the corporate income tax rate. Specifically, we have:

$$YENT = shif_{ent,k} \cdot WK \cdot QKS$$

$$ENTSAV = (1 - ti_{ent})YENT$$

Assuming a dynamic recursive process for capital, the study introduces a dynamic structure to characterize it. Total capital formation is determined by investments from the young and investments in deferred personal pensions, while the allocation of investments among industry sectors is assumed to be exogenously determined by the economic structure:

$$QKS = QKS_{-1} \cdot (1 - \delta) + I^y + SH^y_{pp}$$

⑥ Government Sector

It is assumed that government revenues derive from value-added taxes on the circulation of goods, corporate income taxes, import tariffs, and social insurance contributions levied on the young. Government expenditure consists of government consumption, transfer payments to enterprises, and transfers to the elderly. Government consumption is equal to the portion of expenditure allocated for goods consumption and is exogenously determined. Government behavior can be characterized by:

$$YG = \sum\nolimits_a (tval_a \cdot WL \cdot QLD_a + tvak_a \cdot WK \cdot QKD_a)$$
$$+ti_h \cdot WL \cdot QLS + ti_{ent} \cdot YENT + \sum\nolimits_c tm_c \cdot pwm_c \cdot QM_c \cdot EXR$$

$$EG = \sum_a PQ_a \cdot \overline{QG}_a + transfer_{hg} + transfer_{ent,g}$$

It is assumed that the government is not required to balance its annual budget. The difference between revenues and expenditures represents net government savings, and the ratio of negative savings to total output—the deficit rate—serves as an indicator of fiscal pressure.

$$\mathcal{GSAV} = \mathcal{YG} - \mathcal{EG}$$

⑦ Pension Module

The pension module in this study is designed to compare the effects of pension reforms under a partially funded system with those of the third-pillar personal pension system in the context of population aging. Under the partially funded system, revenue for the social pooling pension comes from contributions by the young and government subsidies for social insurance, whereas expenditures consist of pension benefits paid to the elderly, that is:

$$penrev^{go} = \theta_1 WL \cdot QLS + transfr_{h,g} = transfr_{h,gov} y_h$$

For the personal account component, an elderly individual's personal account income depends on the accumulation from the previous period:

$$SH^o_s = SH^o_{-1,s}$$

Under a fully funded personal pension system, pension income depends entirely on the contributions to personal pensions in the prior period:

$$SH^0_{pp} = SH^0_{-1,pp} \cdot shift_{-1,pp,k} \cdot WK_{-1} \cdot QKS_{-1}$$

⑧ Market Clearing Conditions

The total domestic supply of goods equals the sum of intermediate input usage, household consumption, consumption by various sectors, and government consumption, i.e.:

$$QQ_c = \sum_c QINT_{ca} + \sum_h QH_{ch} + \overline{QINV}_c + QG_c$$

The demand for labor equals its supply, and the demand for capital equals its supply:

$$\sum_a QLD_a = QLS$$

$$\sum_a QKD_a = QKS$$

⑨ International Trade Balance

The total value of imported goods equals the sum of the value of exported goods and net capital inflows, i.e.:

$$\sum_c pwm_c \cdot QM_c = \sum_a pwe_c \cdot QE_c + FSAV$$

Assuming a fixed exchange rate system in a closed economy, with FSAV as an endogenous variable and EXR exogenously determined:

$$EXR = \overline{EXR}$$

⑩ Constraint Conditions

Considering the neoclassical macroeconomic closure conditions, it is assumed that the government budget balance, the wage rate, the capital rate, and the prices in production activities are each equal to their endowment values:

$$GSAV = \overline{GSAV}$$

$$WL = \overline{WL}$$

$$WK = \overline{WK}$$

$$PA = \overline{PA}$$

According to Walras' law in general equilibrium models, this should equal zero, and the investment–savings identity is expressed as:

$$ENIV = (1 - \text{mpc})[YH - (1 - ti_h) \cdot WL \cdot QLS] + ENTSAV + GSAV + EXR \cdot FSAV + WALRAS$$

(2) Pension Balance Forecast Analysis

Figure 3.1 summarizes the impact of different aging scenarios on the macroeconomy over the next 30 years, as assessed in Chapter 1. Numerical simulation results indicate that population aging exerts a profound impact on macroeconomic growth rates; under slow, moderate, and rapid aging scenarios, the average annual growth rate of real GDP over the next 30 years is 2.99%, 1.93%, and –1.02%, respectively. In the baseline scenario (moderate aging), China's GDP growth rate continues to decline during the observation period, approaching a zero-growth level around 2050, and subsequently turning negative. In the most pessimistic scenario, the economic slowdown induced by labor force shocks is the fastest, with the gap in growth rates compared to the baseline scenario widening continuously; between 2020 and 2040, economic growth declines rapidly, with the growth rate turning negative around 2030, coinciding with an inflection point in the growth rate. In contrast, under a slow aging scenario, the impact on the economy is relatively modest, with growth rates persistently hovering around 3% and the negative impact of population aging on the economy exhibiting a diminishing trend.

Furthermore, an analysis from the perspective of industrial structure shows that, as the process of population aging accelerates, households' optimal consumption

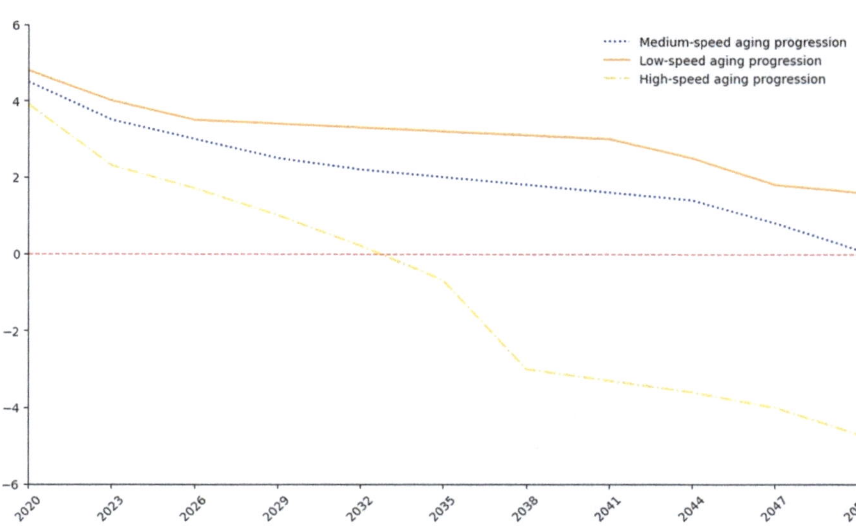

Fig. 3.1 Presents simulation results and comparisons of GDP growth rates under different scenarios from 2020 to 2050

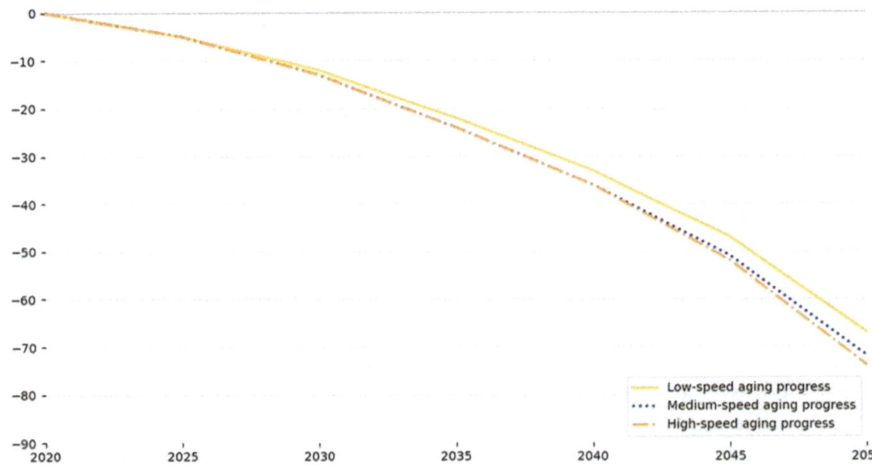

Fig. 3.2 Also presents simulation results and comparisons of pension revenue–expenditure balances under different scenarios from 2020 to 2050

and investment decisions change accordingly. The decline in the labor supply is primarily manifested in a reallocation effect among heterogeneous labor-intensive industries: effective labor supply declines in agriculture and manufacturing, whereas labor absorption in the tertiary sector—represented by resident services and public utilities—improves. In terms of sectoral output, most industries exhibit a downward trend in their contribution to GDP. Sectors such as food processing, power and gas industries, and consumer goods manufacturing are the most severely affected by the impact of aging. Although the construction industry can maintain a positive contribution to GDP, its marginal contribution shows a declining trend over time. In addition, in the financial sector, due to factors such as declining social risk appetite and lower rates of return on industrial investments, the industry's contribution to GDP shows a significant downward trend (Fig. 3.2).

From the perspective of the impact of varying aging rates on pension revenue and expenditure, simulations indicate that under the baseline scenario, China's pension revenue–expenditure gap is –0.37 trillion yuan in 2025. This gap then gradually widens, accelerating from 2030 to approximately 8.63 trillion yuan, and it expands to 70.11 trillion yuan by 2050, posing a severe challenge to government fiscal sustainability. Under different scenarios prior to 2035, the impact of varying aging scenarios on the pension balance shows relatively minor differences; the gap under the rapid-aging scenario is 3.14% larger and that under the slow-aging scenario is 4.1% smaller than in the moderate-aging scenario. However, as aging deepens further, with declines in disposable incomes and consumption levels in the household sector, and with labor shortages exerting stronger negative impacts on industrial output, by 2050 the pension gap under the rapid-aging scenario expands to 7.38% above that in the moderate case, whereas under the slow-aging scenario it is 6.96% below.

(3) Policy Effect Analysis of Pension System Reforms

Based on the aforementioned CGE model analytical framework, which embeds pension system parameters within an endogenous macroeconomic system, this section simulates the overall impact of pension system adjustments under a rapid-aging scenario and analyzes the sustainability effects of different types of pension reforms.

(A) Policy Simulation Scenario 1: Increasing the Pension Contribution Rate of Households.

Table 3.2 illustrates that, under various aging depth scenarios, an increase of 10% in government pension premiums for the household sector yields positive economic effects at the current level of aging (2020 aging level). In the current demographic context, raising the pension contribution level for households contributes 0.002% to real GDP growth, boosts investment by 0.097%, reduces consumption (due to changes in households' optimal decision-making), and—affected by an appreciation of the exchange rate—yields a real export growth contribution of 0.014%. However, under deep-aging conditions (2050 aging level), the same pension policy imposes a clearly negative impact, with a contribution to real GDP of –0.020%. Although the supplement to pensions expands the space for government investment expenditure, contributing 0.017% to economic output, the negative effect on household consumption is more pronounced at –1.037%. Overall, increasing household contributions provides only limited short-term stimulus to the economy while its adverse economic effects intensify as population aging deepens.

(B) Policy Simulation Scenario 2: Reducing the Pension Replacement Level for Households.

Table 3.3 shows the simulation results for maintaining pension sustainability by lowering the government pension replacement level by 10%. The data indicate that, under deep-aging conditions, lowering the pension replacement level can effectively mitigate the negative impact of labor force declines, contributing 0.01% to GDP growth. However, overall, this policy reduces social welfare; household welfare decreases by 63,540 units, thereby reducing the current disposable income of the

Table 3.2 Main macro-economic changes under an increased household pension contribution rate

Macroeconomic variable (%)	2020 aging level	2050 aging level
Real GDP	0.002	–0.020
Investment	0.097	0.017
Consumption	–0.811	–1.037
Imports	–0.087	–0.002
Exports	0.014	–0.002
Exchange rate	0.003	–0.053
Government revenue	0.127	–0.281
Inflation rate	0.004	–0.019

Table 3.3 Policy simulation scenario 3: delaying the retirement age

Macroeconomic variable (%)	2020 aging level	2050 aging level
Real GDP	–0.002	0.001
Investment	0.133	0.087
Consumption	–0.211	–0.084
Imports	–0.017	0.007
Exports	–0.025	0.01
Exchange rate	0.006	–0.003
Government revenue	0.024	–0.010
Inflation rate	0.004	–0.002

elderly, although its negative effect on consumption gradually diminishes in the long run.

Table 3.4 shows that, starting from 2020, raising the retirement age from 60 to 65 produces a more pronounced positive contribution to GDP under deep-aging conditions, with an impact of 0.01%. However, by 2050 the economy still suffers from deep aging, and overall economic performance enters negative territory. The differences in policy impact are mainly reflected in changes in household consumption and exports; for example, in 2020, market consumption and exports increased by 0.32% and 0.037%, respectively. Nevertheless, as population aging deepens, this policy fails to fundamentally improve the environment for economic development.

Policy Simulation Scenario 4: Increasing the Proportion of Deferred Personal Pensions through Higher Tax Deferral

Table 3.5 shows that by increasing the proportion of personal pensions by 3% per annum, the initial stimulative effect on the economy from the development of personal pensions is not significant, primarily due to its relatively small proportional size, which is insufficient to generate effective support for the economy through tax deferral and investment incentives. However, as the level of aging increases, the advantages of this policy gradually emerge. By 2050, owing to the improvement

Table 3.4 Main macro-economic changes under delayed retirement

Macroeconomic variable (%)	2020 aging level	2050 aging level
Real GDP	0.05	–0.015
Investment	0.81	0.153
Consumption	0.32	–0.069
Imports	–0.013	0.017
Exports	0.037	0.02
Exchange rate	0.005	–0.004
Government revenue	0.004	–0.030
Inflation rate	0.005	–0.001

Table 3.5 Main economic changes under increased proportion of personal pensions

Macroeconomic variable (%)	2020 aging level	2050 aging level
Real GDP	0.01	0.001
Investment	0.33	0.413
Consumption	0.211	–0.041
Imports	–0.017	0.007
Exports	–0.025	0.01
Exchange rate	0.006	–0.003
Government revenue	0.024	–0.010
Inflation rate	0.004	–0.002

in younger households' pension reserve incomes resulting from pension system reforms, the negative side-effect on consumption is minimized, and the economy is able to maintain a positive growth rate of 0.001.

In summary, among the pension system reforms implemented to address population aging, the promotion of the third-pillar personal pensions yields the highest economic contribution, followed by delayed retirement. Simultaneously, as the share of personal pensions in the overall pension system increases, it becomes possible to lower the replacement rate of the first-pillar government pensions, thereby providing a dual boost to the economy.

Chapter 4
Future Reform Directions and Impacts

4.1 The Implications of Pension System Transformation

4.1.1 The Core Logic of Pension System Transformation: A Paradigm Reconstruction from Intergenerational Solidarity to Individual Accumulation

The essence of pension system transformation entails a fundamental restructuring of the resource allocation mechanism for retirement provision, characterized by a transition from an intergenerational transfer model centered on the pay-as-you-go system toward an individual accumulation model based on a funded scheme. The pay-as-you-go system sustains retirement benefits through contributions from the current working population, with its institutional logic predicated on the assumption of a stable demographic structure, achieving intergenerational solidarity through social redistribution. In contrast, the funded system introduces market mechanisms, forming a pool of pension assets through individual account accumulation, achieving preservation and appreciation of capital through capital market operations, and emphasizing the direct correlation between individual responsibility and returns.

International experience indicates that the primary impetus for this transformation stems from the impact of population aging on system sustainability. For instance, the Social Security Trust Fund in the United States, which operates on a pay-as-you-go basis, is projected to be depleted by 2035, whereas Chile's funded system reform initiated in 1981, through the linkage of individual accounts with capital markets, not only alleviated fiscal pressure but also drove the ratio of pension assets to GDP from 3 to 85%. This model conversion involves not only a change in financing methods but also a redefinition of the boundaries of responsibility among government, enterprises, and individuals, shifting from "government-backed guarantees" to "multi-stakeholder risk-sharing."

T. Wang et al., *China's Pension Reform*, Contributions to Finance and Accounting,
https://doi.org/10.1007/978-981-95-0103-8_4

4.1.2 The Unique Context of China's Pension System Transformation: The Dual Properties of the Combined Model

China's pension system transformation exhibits distinctive "dual-track" characteristics—a hybrid model that combines social pooling with individual accounts. This design originated from the 1997 "Decision of the State Council on Establishing a Unified Basic Pension Insurance System for Enterprise Employees," aimed at balancing social equity with market efficiency. As of the end of 2024, the accumulated balance of the urban employee basic pension insurance fund reached 6.5 trillion yuan, with individual account bookkeeping entries accounting for 45%; however, the actual investment operation scale constituted only 20%, with the remainder held in low-yield bank deposits, highlighting the structural contradiction between "nominal accounts" and "actual accumulation."

This institutional design, with its historical path dependency, has exposed problems such as intensified intergenerational transfer pressure on pooling accounts and the "empty account operation" of individual accounts against the backdrop of accelerated population aging (with the population aged 60 and above exceeding 310 million). The disparity in pension benefits between urban and rural residents has reached 3.4 times, with the average monthly pension for residents at only 240 yuan, less than 1/14 of the employee pension, reflecting an imbalance between the redistribution function and savings incentives within the system. Guo Shuqing, in his 2025 economic situation report, emphasized the need to restructure the institutional framework through "layered design and market participation," retaining the baseline security function of the pay-as-you-go system while activating the capital allocation efficiency of the funded system.

4.1.3 The Deeper Challenges of Transformation: Interest Reconfiguration and Risk Prevention During System Transition

The essence of pension system transformation lies in the redefinition of the social contract, involving multi-stakeholder interest adjustments and risk prevention. From international experience, the transitional costs primarily include the inheritance of old system liabilities, operational costs of the new system, and benefit assurance during the transition period. Chile absorbed the liabilities of the old system by issuing "recognition bonds," which accounted for 40% of GDP and were amortized over 30 years; Poland adopted a Notional Defined Contribution (NDC) system, simulating funded system returns through notional interest rates, thus avoiding substantial transitional costs.

China's transformation faces dual constraints of "growing old before growing rich" and the urban–rural dichotomy: in 2024, the per capita GDP was only

US$13,000, below the aging threshold of US$20,000 in developed countries, while rural residents accounted for 60% of the insured population, with an average contribution of only 800 yuan, far below the 12,000 yuan for urban employees. Furthermore, insufficient capital market maturity leads to concentration of risks in the funded system; for example, stocks constituted over 50% of Chilean pension investment portfolios for an extended period, resulting in a 30% shrinkage of individual account assets during the 2008 financial crisis. These structural contradictions necessitate that the transformation balance equity and efficiency, establishing a diversified mechanism of "government baseline guarantees + market operations + risk buffering."

4.2 Learning from System Transition Experiences

4.2.1 China's Pension Integration Practice: A Breakthrough from "Dual-Track System" to "Combined Pooling and Individual Accounts"

A critical step in China's pension system transition has been breaking down the "dual-track" disparities between government institutions and enterprises. The 2015 *Decision of the State Council on the Reform of the Pension Insurance System for Employees of Government and Public Institutions* established a framework of "one unification, five synchronizations," namely, unifying the basic pension insurance system, simultaneously reforming the salary system of government and public institutions, and improving the transfer and continuation of pension insurance relationships. Following the reform, personnel in government and public institutions implemented a model combining social pooling with individual accounts, with joint contributions from both units and individuals, alongside the synchronous establishment of an occupational pension system, resolving long-standing issues of inequitable benefits and barriers to talent mobility.

By 2022, nationwide pooling had been achieved for enterprise employees and government institution pension insurance, the minimum standard for rural and urban residents' basic pensions increased by 19.4%, and the personal pension system was officially launched. For instance, Zhejiang Province took the lead in improving the rural and urban residents' pension insurance system in 2014, boosting the coverage rate to 95% through fiscal subsidies and contribution incentives. These practices demonstrate that system integration must be predicated on "baseline equity," reducing group disparities through phased implementation and differentiated subsidies, while strengthening the market-oriented operational capacity of funds, as evidenced by the basic pension insurance fund's entrusted investment achieving an annualized return of 5.3%, outperforming the inflation rate by 2.5 percentage points.

4.2.2 Adaptability Modification of International Models: From Latin American Experiences to European Multi-Pillar Systems

(1) Insights from Latin American Funded Models and Their Localization

The success of Chile's fully funded reform lies in the combination of individual account choice and stringent supervision, though caution is warranted regarding its excessive reliance on capital markets (with equities exceeding 50%). China can draw on its "incentive compatibility" mechanisms, allowing individual account funds to be allocated across the life cycle, while establishing a risk reserve system that activates compensation mechanisms when fund returns fall below the risk-free rate by more than 2 percentage points. For flexible employment groups, a "tiered contribution" scheme could be designed, such as ride-hailing drivers contributing 5% of monthly income below 5,000 yuan, with a 30% government subsidy to incentivize long-term participation.

(2) Drawing on and Innovating from European Multi-Pillar Models

Germany's "mini-pension" contribution incentive mechanism for flexibly employed individuals provides insights for encouraging participation among China's new-economy workers. A "baseline + incentive" structure could be established for basic pensions, dividing residents' pensions into a nationally standardized "baseline component" and an "incentive component" linked to contribution years, with basic pensions increasing by 5% for each additional year of contribution. Sweden's Notional Defined Contribution (NDC) system, with its "bookkeeping rate linked to social average wage" mechanism, offers a reference for substantiating China's individual accounts; the accounting interest rate could be dynamically adjusted (not less than 3%) to enhance the system's attractiveness, while permitting account balance inheritance to address the "empty account" challenge.

(3) Exploring the Adaptability of Asian Provident Fund Models

Singapore's Central Provident Fund system, with its "mandatory savings + individual accounts" model, provides a reference for the development of China's third pillar. Linkages between personal pension accounts and innovative products such as reverse mortgage pensions could be promoted, allowing account funds to be invested in commercial pension insurance and target-date pension funds, with the tax preference ratio increased from 12 to 20%. As of 2024, China's third pillar scale was approximately 8 trillion yuan, representing less than 5% of GDP, necessitating policy guidance and product innovation to narrow the gap with the United States' 35%, thereby constructing a multi-tiered system of "government-guaranteed baseline, enterprise supplementation, and individual savings.“

4.2.3 Basic Orientations for Future Reform

The core objective of China's pension system reform is to construct a sustainable, equitable multi-pillar system adapted to population aging trends. Combining domestic and international experiences with practical challenges, future reforms need to achieve breakthroughs in the following directions:

(1) Constructing a Multi-Tiered, Multi-Pillar Pension Insurance System

Drawing on international experiences, particularly the transition models of OECD and Latin American countries, China should further strengthen its "three-pillar" framework. The first pillar (basic pension insurance) needs to consolidate its function of providing basic security and establishing a safety net, gradually reducing the benefit disparities between urban and rural areas as well as among different groups; the second pillar (enterprise/occupational pensions) needs to expand coverage and enhance protection levels; the third pillar (individual savings-type pension insurance) needs to accelerate development through tax incentives, product innovations, and other policies. Simultaneously, the exploration of establishing a "zero pillar" (fiscally supported minimum guarantee) and a fourth pillar (non-economic support, such as family support and medical services) would create a comprehensive protection network.

(2) Optimizing Fiscal Responsibility and State-Owned Asset Transfer Mechanisms

Faced with fiscal pressures from population aging, there is a need to further deepen fiscal subsidy and state-owned asset transfer reforms. According to projections, the employee basic pension insurance fund is expected to face a deficit around 2035, with the resident pension insurance fund's dependence on fiscal subsidies being even more prominent. Consideration could be given to increasing the proportion of state-owned capital transfers (e.g., gradually raising the proportion of central enterprises and financial institutions' equity transfers from 10 to 20%) and establishing specialized investment companies for operations to ensure fund preservation and appreciation. Additionally, there is a need to clarify central and local fiscal responsibilities, establishing dynamic adjustment mechanisms to avoid payment pressures on local governments due to population outflows.

(3) Advancing Nationwide Pooling and Coverage Expansion of Basic Pension Insurance

While nationwide pooling has been achieved for urban employees' pension insurance, there remain issues of significant regional disparities and low pooling levels in residents' pension insurance. Future efforts should accelerate nationwide pooling of rural and urban residents' pension insurance, progressively unifying contribution standards and benefit adjustment mechanisms. Concurrently, innovative participation methods should be developed for flexible employment personnel and new-economy practitioners to expand system coverage. For instance, allowing flexibly employed individuals to independently select their contribution base and simplifying transfer and continuation procedures would enhance the system's attractiveness.

(4) Strengthening Market-Oriented Investment and Risk Management

The investment return rate of China's basic pension insurance fund balance has remained relatively low over the long term —for example, the employee fund return rate was only 2.2% in 2024—necessitating further relaxation of investment restrictions and the introduction of market competition. Chile's "private pension company" model could be referenced, allowing funds to invest in diversified assets such as stocks, bonds, and infrastructure, with enhanced returns through professional institutional management. Simultaneously, risk diversification mechanisms should be established, such as a national pension investment risk reserve fund, to avoid excessive impacts on funds from single market fluctuations.

(5) Promoting Delayed Retirement and Incentive Mechanism Reforms

Population aging leads to reduced labor supply, necessitating delayed retirement policies to alleviate pension payment pressures. A "flexible retirement system" could be adopted, allowing workers to choose their retirement age based on health and economic conditions, complemented by tax incentives or pension supplementation mechanisms. Furthermore, introducing "more contributions, more benefits; longer contributions, more benefits" incentive mechanisms in basic pension insurance would encourage residents to increase their contribution levels, thereby enhancing individual account accumulation.

Chapter 5
Policy Recommendations for the Development of Personal Pensions

5.1 The Significance of Personal Pension Development for China's Pension System Transition

5.1.1 Alleviating Pressure on Basic Pension Insurance and Optimizing the Three-Pillar Structure

China faces structural challenges from the combined effects of deep population aging and declining fertility, which have highlighted the pressure on the long-term balance of the basic pension insurance fund. In 2023, nationwide expenditures from the enterprise employees' basic pension insurance fund reached 6.2 trillion yuan, with fiscal subsidies accounting for over 15%. The establishment of the personal pension system, by attracting voluntary participation through market-oriented mechanisms, can effectively mitigate payment pressures on the first pillar. By the end of 2024, the number of personal pension accounts in pilot cities exceeded 50 million, covering approximately 3.5% of the working population. Calculated at the annual maximum contribution limit of 12,000 yuan, this could theoretically generate a supplementary pension fund pool exceeding 600 billion yuan. This collaborative mechanism, integrating both government and market approaches, not only aligns with international pension reform trends but also provides crucial support for China's transition from a pay-as-you-go system to a multi-pillar model.

T. Wang et al., *China's Pension Reform*, Contributions to Finance and Accounting,
https://doi.org/10.1007/978-981-95-0103-8_5

5.1.2 Enhancing Retirement Security Levels and Addressing Longevity Risk

China's current basic pension replacement rate is approximately 45%, which falls substantially below the 55% warning threshold recommended by the International Labor Organization. Personal pensions, as the third pillar, can significantly increase retirement income through tax-deferral incentive mechanisms. For instance, a middle-income individual with a monthly income of 15,000 yuan who contributes 12,000 yuan annually to a personal pension—assuming an average annual investment return of 5%—would accumulate approximately 840,000 yuan after 30 years, providing a supplementary monthly income of about 4,200 yuan after retirement. This institutional design not only strengthens individual responsibility for retirement planning but also achieves the preservation and appreciation of pension assets through market-oriented investment, effectively hedging against inflation and longevity risks.

5.1.3 Promoting Pension Financial Innovation and Facilitating Capital Market Development

The implementation of the personal pension system has accelerated innovation in pension financial products. As of April 2024, 746 specialized products had been launched, encompassing four major categories: wealth management, savings, insurance, and funds. Among these, pension target funds (Y-shares) exceeded 50 billion yuan in scale, with target-date funds employing life-cycle strategies accounting for over 60%. These products, through long-term closed operations, provide stable long-term capital to the capital markets. The U.S. experience demonstrates that Individual Retirement Accounts (IRAs) hold more than 40% of mutual fund assets, driving the institutionalization process of American equities. If funds from China's personal pensions continue to enter the market, they will optimize the structure of capital market investors, promote the dissemination of value investment principles, and form a virtuous cycle of "pension asset appreciation—capital market development—real economy growth."

5.1.4 Resolving System Transition Challenges and Improving the Multi-tiered Pension System

China's pension system is undergoing a historic transformation from a "single-pillar" to a "three-pillar collaborative" structure. Through an account-based design, personal pensions transcend the regional and occupational limitations of traditional pension insurance, providing a retirement security pathway for flexible workers and those employed in new economic forms. By the end of 2023, the number of flexibly employed individuals with insurance coverage had reached 230 million, representing 40% of the urban employed population. The personal pension system, through tax incentives and product innovation, will effectively activate the retirement savings demand of this substantial group. Simultaneously, by establishing conversion channels between the second and third pillars, allowing enterprise annuities to be transferred into personal pension accounts, the portability and attractiveness of the system can be significantly enhanced, accelerating the cross-pillar integration of pension assets.

5.1.5 Responding to Demographic Transition and Cultivating a Long-Term Savings Culture

Faced with the severe reality of a total fertility rate that has fallen to 1.09, the family's function in supporting the elderly continues to weaken. The personal pension system, through mandatory savings and tax incentives, can effectively compensate for deficiencies in intergenerational family support capabilities. The successful experience of Japan's iDeCo plan demonstrates that differentiated tax incentives (such as a combination of EET and TEE models) can accommodate the needs of different income groups. If China further optimizes its preferential tax policies by implementing direct fiscal subsidies for low-income groups and raising contribution limits for high-income groups, the inclusiveness of the system will be significantly enhanced. Additionally, reducing choice costs through "default investment portfolio" mechanisms, combined with investor education to improve financial literacy, can gradually cultivate residents' awareness of long-term retirement planning, thereby building strategic resources to address deep population aging.

5.2 Problems in the Development of Personal Pensions in China

5.2.1 Insufficient Policy Precision and Inclusiveness

The current personal pension system employs a one-size-fits-all policy design; the annual contribution cap of 12,000 yuan and uniform tax incentive model are inadequate to accommodate differentiated needs. Data show that as of March 2025, the number of personal pension accounts has exceeded 70 million, yet the actual contribution rate is below 30%, reflecting limited appeal among middle- and low-income groups. The prevailing tax incentive scheme adopts an EET model, which fails to provide substantial incentives for individuals earning less than 5,000 yuan per month, while high-income groups face diminishing marginal utility. For example, individuals with a monthly income of 30,000 yuan save only about 1,800 yuan in taxes through personal pensions—well below their expected returns from investment and financial products. Moreover, the policy design does not fully account for the enrollment needs of special groups such as flexible workers and new-economy practitioners, resulting in structural gaps in coverage.

5.2.2 Lagging Product Innovation and Severe Homogeneity

Although nearly a thousand products have been launched since the policy was implemented, there is a pronounced imbalance in the product mix. As of March 2025, savings-type products account for nearly 50% of the market, whereas equity-based products constitute only 30%. The average annualized return of pension target funds (FOFs) is below 4%, underperforming market expectations. Significant product homogeneity is evident, with bank wealth management, funds, and insurance products exhibiting minimal differences in investment strategies and risk-return profiles, thereby failing to meet the needs of investors differing in age and risk preference. For instance, long-term investment products targeting the post-1980s and post-1990s cohorts lack innovation, and existing products are generally characterized by excessively long lock-up periods and insufficient liquidity.

5.2.3 Limited Account Flexibility and Restricted Usage Scenarios

The current account system stipulates that funds can only be withdrawn after retirement, lacking flexible mechanisms to address unexpected needs. Although the 2024 policy added provisions for early withdrawal in cases of major illness or unemployment, practical implementation still suffers from complex procedures and stringent approval requirements. Surveys indicate that 72% of respondents believe the lack of emergency functions in the accounts reduces their willingness to participate. Moreover, a system for inter-account connectivity has not yet been established; for instance, the second-pillar enterprise annuities and the third-pillar personal pensions cannot be transferred between accounts, and linking with other funds such as the housing provident fund remains difficult, thereby constraining the efficiency of overall pension asset management.

5.2.4 Weak Investor Education System

A lack of financial literacy has emerged as a major barrier to promoting the system. Specialized research conducted in 2025 demonstrates that only 38% of investors can correctly understand the tax incentive rules associated with personal pensions, and 55% of respondents report confusion regarding product selection. Current investor education primarily relies on fragmented promotion by financial institutions, lacking a systematic and authoritative educational platform. Young people, in particular, exhibit a weak awareness of retirement planning—only 16% of those aged 25–35 have formulated a clear pension investment plan, which is significantly below levels observed in developed countries. Additionally, some financial institutions exhibit an overemphasis on sales, leading to inadequate investor awareness of product risks.

5.2.5 *Inadequate Coordination in the Regulatory Framework*

A multi-agency coordinated regulatory system has not yet been fully established, resulting in regulatory gaps and opportunities for arbitrage. For example, pension trust products have not been incorporated into the institutional framework, and certain high-risk products are illicitly sold by unlicensed entities. There are also deficiencies in the fund security assurance mechanisms—an incident of customer information leakage in 2024 on one platform raised public concerns about account security. At the same time, product evaluation standards are inconsistent, and the risk classifications for different types of products lack comparability, thereby impeding the scientific basis for investor decision-making.

5.2.6 *Lack of Motivation Among Market Participants*

Financial institutions tend to adopt a "scale-oriented rather than service-oriented" approach in product development, and homogeneous competition has resulted in insufficient investment in innovation. Bank channels are heavily reliant on the sale of savings-type products, fund companies face pressure on management fee income, and insurance companies are constrained by their long-term fund management capabilities. Some small and medium-sized financial institutions, lacking professional talent and system support, are unable to offer personalized services. Increased volatility in the capital markets has also aggravated the uncertainty of product returns; in 2024, the average drawdown of equity-based pension products reached 12%, thereby undermining investor confidence.

5.3 International Experience and Lessons Learned

Amidst the rapid acceleration of global population aging, the development of China's personal pension system must, while rooted in domestic practice, draw deeply on mature international experiences. Although China's personal pension system has already been promoted nationwide, there remains significant room for improvement in areas such as product design, account flexibility, and tax incentives. An analysis of the exemplary practices of countries like the United States, Japan, and Chile can help distill reform pathways with high reference value.

5.3.1 Differentiated Design of Tax Incentive Policies

International experience indicates that the precision of tax incentives directly impacts system participation. The U.S. IRA program implements differential tax policies for various income groups: traditional IRAs adopt an EET model (tax-exempt contributions and investment earnings with taxation on withdrawal), while Roth IRAs use a TEE model (taxed contributions with tax-free investment earnings and withdrawals); the latter is more favored by middle- and low-income groups due to its tax-free withdrawal phase. Japan offers a tax exemption quota of 20% on investment earnings via NISA accounts, and it provides minors with junior accounts that enjoy a five-year tax-free period, effectively nurturing a culture of pension savings among young people. In contrast, China's current annual contribution cap of 12,000 yuan and a 3% withdrawal tax rate lack sufficient appeal for middle- and low-income earners. Lessons can be drawn from Germany's Li Si Te pension plan, which employs fiscal subsidies as direct transfers to non-taxpayer groups. There is also potential to explore a shift towards an EEE (fully tax-exempt) model along with establishing a dynamic adjustment mechanism linking contribution ceilings to the social average wage.

5.3.2 Construction of a Life-Cycle Account System

Account flexibility is key to enhancing the system's stickiness. In the United States, inter-account transfers between the second and third pillars are permitted, with 95% of IRA assets originating from transfers out of enterprise annuities, and provisions allow for conversion to a Roth IRA near retirement to circumvent tax restrictions. New Zealand's KiwiSaver program has innovated an "auto-enrollment with opt-out" mechanism that covers over 90% of the working-age population and permits the use of account funds for first-home purchases and medical expenses. Currently, China's personal pension accounts are relatively limited in scope and lack a mechanism for familial pooling. It is worth exploring the establishment of a dual-layer structure comprising a "basic account + supplementary account": the basic account would provide a guaranteed return and support emergency withdrawals (e.g., for major health expenses), while the supplementary account would allow for discretionary allocation into higher-risk assets; additionally, a system of family-shared quotas could be introduced to permit joint declarations by spouses, raise contribution ceilings, and implement differentiated subsidies for families with multiple children.

5.3.3 Innovation in a Diversified Product Supply System

Experience from mature markets indicates that product diversity and return stability are central to the sustainability of a system. In the U.S., 41% of IRA assets are allocated to equity funds, generating annualized returns of over 7% through a global asset allocation strategy; in Japan, 39.5% of iDeCo account funds are invested in investment trusts, while NISA accounts encourage allocations to REITs and ETFs. Currently, savings-type products account for nearly half of China's personal pension offerings, with equity-based products constituting less than 30%. There is a need to break new ground in the following areas: first, by involving professional institutions such as the National Social Security Fund and enterprise annuities in product design to develop target-date funds (TDFs) and enhanced-index products; second, by piloting a cross-border investment mechanism that permits allocations in mature market assets such as Hong Kong and U.S. stocks; and third, by exploring pension trust products that leverage the inherent independence of trust assets to achieve intergenerational wealth transfer.

5.3.4 Development of an Intelligent Investment Advisory Service System

The U.S. Department of Labor's QDIA system, implemented in 2006, mandates that employers provide a default investment portfolio for employees who do not actively choose a product, resulting in a 293-fold increase in the scale of target-date funds over a decade. China can learn from this model by establishing a big-data-based intelligent advisory system: by analyzing enrollees' age, income, risk preferences, and other characteristics, the system can automatically match individuals with appropriate life-cycle strategies (for instance, emphasizing equity investments for younger cohorts and shifting toward fixed-income assets as retirement nears); concurrently, a dynamic adjustment mechanism for a white list of products could be instituted, utilizing metrics such as the Sharpe ratio and maximum drawdown for performance evaluation, and eliminating products that fail to achieve long-term returns.

5.3.5 Risk Prevention and the Enhancement of Regulatory Coordination Mechanisms

The Chilean model for private pension management companies (AFPs) raises returns through competitive mechanisms; however, excessive marketing has resulted in management fees accounting for as much as 1.1% of assets. China needs to construct a dual-track system composed of "transparent regulation coupled with consumer education": on the regulatory side, a cross-departmental data-sharing platform should be established to monitor fund flows and product risks in real time; on the investor education side, standardized pension investment knowledge frameworks should be developed, utilizing short videos, comics, and other formats to disseminate concepts such as the power of compounding and asset allocation, and a performance evaluation mechanism for financial institution investor education should be instituted.

5.3.6 Cross-Cycle Application of Policy Tools

Singapore's Central Provident Fund system, which integrates "mandatory savings + insurance + investment," achieves a pension replacement rate of over 60%. China could explore linking its personal pensions with housing provident funds and medical insurance accounts by allowing individuals to transfer their provident fund balances into personal pension accounts to earn higher returns. At the same time, China could also develop health and pension insurance products that integrate with individual medical accounts, thereby forming a comprehensive security system encompassing "savings + healthcare + pensions."

5.4 Policy Recommendations

5.4.1 Establish a Targeted Policy Support System to Broaden Coverage

To address the limitations of the current "one-size-fits-all" policy, it is necessary to develop a differentiated policy framework. It is recommended to dynamically link the contribution cap to residents' income levels. For example, using 30% of the regional average wage as the benchmark, allow the cap of 12,000 yuan to fluctuate within a ±50% range. For high-income groups, implement a tiered tax incentive system that increases the tax-saving ratio from 3 to 5–8%; for middle- and low-income groups, implement dual incentives of a "contribution subsidy plus tax deduction," such as providing a fiscal subsidy of 15% of the contribution amount. Drawing on Japan's NISA initiative, introduce family joint accounts that allow spouses to share a contribution quota of 24,000 yuan, with an additional annual subsidy of 3,000 yuan for families with multiple children.

In terms of expanding coverage, priority should be given to flexible workers and new urban residents. For instance, for gig workers such as couriers and ride-hailing drivers, establish a "per-transaction contribution" mechanism that allows them to choose monthly, quarterly, or annual contributions based on income fluctuations. Drawing on the New Zealand KiwiSaver experience, offer a subsidy equal to 50% of the first-year contribution for recent graduates opening their first account, capped at 6,000 yuan. In the realm of tax administration, promote the implementation of an "individual income tax APP with intelligent forecasting" functionality that automatically generates personalized participation plans, thereby reducing the cost of understanding policy details.

5.4.2 *Innovate Account Management Mechanisms to Enhance Flexibility*

Establish a flexible withdrawal system: allow enrollees aged 55 and above to withdraw up to 10% of the account balance annually for emergency needs such as medical expenses or children's education, with such withdrawals subject to a 5% tax rate. For special circumstances such as major illnesses, allow full withdrawal, exempt from taxation.

(1) **Establish Channels for Multi-account Linkages**

Develop a transfer mechanism between second-pillar enterprise annuities and third-pillar personal pensions, permitting employees to transfer their enterprise annuity balances into their personal pension accounts upon retirement while enjoying tax deferral. Explore the conversion of assets between the housing provident fund and pension accounts, allowing up to 30% of the provident fund balance to be transferred annually into personal pension accounts for long-term investments.

(2) **Optimize the Account Service System**

Promote the concept of a "retirement wealth management account" by integrating products across banks, funds, and insurance sectors to achieve "one account, panoramic management." Establish a whitelist system for product selection, whereby regulatory authorities dynamically evaluate and recommend financial products that satisfy pension requirements.

5.4.3 *Develop a Diversified Product System to Enhance Market Competitiveness*

(1) **Enrich Product Types**

In addition to the existing four product categories, develop new products such as "pension trusts" and "reverse mortgage loans." Permit pension target funds to invest in inflation-hedging assets such as REITs and gold ETFs and raise the foreign asset allocation cap to 20%. Pilot "comprehensive pension protection portfolio products" that combine insurance protection with investment returns.

(2) **Enhance Product Suitability**

Design differentiated products for investors with varying risk preferences. For conservative investors, develop products offering "guaranteed returns plus variable dividends"; for aggressive investors, launch index-linked products tied to major global equity indices. Establish a dynamic life-cycle adjustment mechanism that automatically adjusts the stock–bond allocation ratio based on the investor's age.

(3) **Strengthen Risk Management**

Require retirement wealth management products to establish a risk reserve system by setting aside 20% of management fee revenues as a risk reserve. Introduce third-party custodian mechanisms to ensure that assets are operated independently. For pension target funds, implement a "dual fund manager" system, with at least one manager possessing more than 10 years of investment experience.

5.4.4 Perfect the Investor Education System and Cultivate a Long-Term Investment Philosophy

(1) **Construct a Three-Tiered Education Network**

Incorporate retirement wealth management into high school finance curricula at the basic education level; develop specialized training for corporate employees at the vocational education level; and establish "retirement planning service hubs" at the community level to provide advisory services.

(2) **Innovate Educational Methods**

Utilize virtual reality technology to develop a "retirement planning simulation system," enabling investors to intuitively experience the long-term effects of different investment strategies. Promote the distribution of an "easy-to-understand retirement investment guide" that explains product risk and return characteristics in plain language.

(3) **Establish Incentive Mechanisms**

Grant an additional 1% tax deduction to investors who participate in the personal pension plan continuously for five years. Organize "retirement planning expert" selection activities to recognize and commend investors who successfully realize asset appreciation.

5.4.5 *Improve the Regulatory Coordination Mechanism to Prevent Systemic Risks*

(1) **Establish a Cross-Departmental Regulatory Coordination Committee**

Coordinate policies among departments such as human resources, finance, and the central bank. Implement "transparent (penetrating) regulation" to monitor fund flows in real time. Establish a negative list for pension financial products to clearly define prohibited activities.

(2) **Improve the Information Disclosure System**

Require financial institutions to disclose key information, such as product investment portfolios and fee structures, on a quarterly basis. Establish a product rating system, with dynamic evaluations carried out by independent third-party agencies.

(3) **Construct a Risk Warning System**

Develop a pension financial risk monitoring platform that sets early warning indicators for liquidity risk, credit risk, and other risks. Establish an emergency response mechanism and prepare contingency plans in anticipation of potential redemption risks.

5.4.6 *Promote the Use of Technology to Empower Pension Finance and Enhance Service Efficiency*

(1) **Develop Intelligent Investment Advisory Systems**

Utilize big data analytics to assess enrollees' risk preferences, life-cycle stages, and other characteristics, providing personalized asset allocation recommendations. Establish an AI-driven customer service system that offers 24-hour support for investor inquiries.

(2) **Apply Blockchain Technology**

Develop digital certificates for pension accounts to enable cross-institution information sharing. Leverage smart contracts to automate processes such as contributions and investment operations.

(3) **Explore an Integrated "Pension Finance + Healthcare" Model**

Allow individuals to use their personal pension account funds to purchase commercial health insurance, thereby achieving a "medical and pension integration" model. Develop a "health management points" system that adjusts investment strategies based on the individual's health status.

Chapter 6
The Technological Development of Artificial Intelligence and the Fintech Revolution

6.1 The Technological Development of Artificial Intelligence and the Fintech Revolution

6.1.1 Core Technological Development: A Paradigm Breakthrough from Single-Modality to Intelligent Agents

(1) **Embodied Intelligence: Innovations in the Interaction Between the Physical and Digital Worlds**

Embodied AI, as an important direction in the development of artificial intelligence, is reshaping service models in the financial sector. This technology embeds intelligent systems into physical entities or virtual carriers, enabling them to perceive the environment, make autonomous decisions, and execute actions. For example, in pension management scenarios, embodied AI can be applied to smart customer service robots that leverage natural language processing (NLP) and voice recognition technologies to promptly address inquiries about account information and benefit calculations, while incorporating simulated body language (e.g., gestural interactions of virtual avatars) to enhance service affinity. More sophisticated applications include IoT-based health monitoring for retirees, where wearable devices collect physiological data and the embodied AI system automatically analyzes health risks and triggers early warnings, thereby providing data support for the dynamic adjustment of pension accounts.

(2) **Unified Multimodal Large Models: A Cognitive Upgrade that Breaks Data Barriers**

Unified multimodal large models, represented by OmniGen, are achieving deep integration of multidimensional data such as text, images, and videos. OmniGen, through its dual-modal "text-image" input architecture, can handle diverse tasks

T. Wang et al., *China's Pension Reform*, Contributions to Finance and Accounting,
https://doi.org/10.1007/978-981-95-0103-8_6

without relying on additional modules (such as ControlNet). For instance, it can combine textual descriptions of pension policy documents with visual representations of insured individuals to generate personalized retirement planning schemes. Its training data encompass 100 million images, including open-source datasets (such as Recap-DataComp and LAION-Aesthetic) and synthetic data (annotated via InternVL2). Through a multi-stage training strategy—beginning with broad semantic matching and then optimizing aesthetic quality—it achieves semantic understanding of complex financial scenarios. In the pension sector, such models can be used to analyze the visual correlations between historical contribution data and population aging trends, thereby assisting policymakers in intuitively assessing the effects of different reform schemes.

(3) **Intelligent Agents: A New Form of Financial Service with Autonomous Decision-Making**

AI intelligent agents are evolving from mere tools to entities capable of autonomous decision-making. In the field of financial regulation, intelligent agents can monitor pension fund transactions in real time, identify abnormal patterns—such as irregular high-frequency trading or unusual fund flows—using machine learning algorithms, automatically trigger risk warnings, and generate compliance reports. For example, the "AI Grid Manager" in Hangzhou, trained on more than 5,000 policy documents, can respond within three seconds to public concerns such as delays in newborn vaccination schedules. Transferred to pension services, such technology can automate processes like insured registration and benefit claims. More advanced intelligent agents possess dynamic strategy adjustment capabilities; for instance, they can automatically optimize pension investment portfolios in response to fluctuations in capital markets, thereby enhancing returns while ensuring safety.

6.1.2 Fundamental Support Technologies: Reconstructing the Underlying Data and Algorithms

(1) **Data Elements and Governance: Building a Trustworthy Digital Foundation**

Data, as the core productive element of AI development, is undergoing a governance transformation within the pension sector. The National Financial Supervision Administration has proposed technical principles on "data security and consumer privacy protection," promoting the establishment of federated learning mechanisms among financial institutions to enable cross-institutional data sharing without compromising privacy. For example, in pension actuarial models, data from multiple provinces and municipalities can be jointly used to train models, with each participant contributing only encrypted parameters rather than raw data, thereby enhancing model accuracy while meeting data security requirements. Simultaneously, regions such as

Beijing are promoting the market-oriented allocation of data elements by establishing fintech clusters (with over 1,800 companies, including 564 high-tech enterprises), exploring the integrated use of pension data with external data such as macroeconomic indicators and demographic statistics to support long-term trend forecasting.

(2) **Inference Optimization and Algorithm Enhancement: Dual Breakthroughs in Efficiency and Security**

Algorithmic optimization is primarily manifested in model compression and inference acceleration. For instance, the Phi-3 small language model employs a lightweight design (using techniques such as quantized training and pruning), maintaining high semantic understanding while reducing computational resource consumption, making it suitable for edge deployment in pension systems, such as self-service terminals in community service centers. In terms of security algorithms, adversarial training techniques are utilized to enhance model robustness and defend against adversarial attacks on pension data (such as fraudulent insured record manipulations intended to deceive AI approval systems). Academician Zhang Bo of the Chinese Academy of Sciences has pointed out that large models may produce "uncontrollable and untrustworthy" outputs, necessitating the use of trusted AI technologies (such as explainable neural networks) to enhance decision-making transparency and ensure fairness in the implementation of pension policies.

6.1.3 The Frontier of Fintech Development: A New Ecosystem Emphasizing Both Intelligent Driving and Security

(1) **Intelligent Driving: Reshaping the Value Chain of Financial Services**

In pension businesses, intelligent driving technology has penetrated multiple segments:

① **Intelligent Investment Advisory.** By leveraging user data such as age, risk preferences, and contribution history, systems can generate customized investment portfolios; for example, combining target-date funds with AI algorithms to dynamically adjust the asset allocation between equities and fixed-income instruments.

② **Risk Assessment.** By employing graph neural networks (GNN) to analyze the interrelationships among participants in enterprise annuities, the system can identify potential credit risks, such as the transmission effects of a corporate default on downstream pension plans within an industrial chain.

③ **Customer Service.** AI-powered customer service robots provide 24/7 support, utilizing affective computing technologies to perceive users' emotions and offer empathetic responses to inquiries regarding pension benefit adjustments, thereby enhancing user experience.

Digital currency technologies provide innovative pathways for cross-border pension settlements and benefit disbursements. The smart contract capabilities of digital renminbi can facilitate conditional pension payments; for instance, automatically triggering benefit disbursement upon meeting conditions such as "attaining retirement age and a cumulative contribution period of 15 years," thus reducing risks associated with manual interventions. In cross-border pension scenarios, blockchain-based digital currency settlement systems can complete real-time currency conversions, thereby mitigating losses from exchange rate fluctuations. The Beijing Fintech Demonstration Zone has piloted the application of digital renminbi in the pension sector, using smart contracts to enable precise allocation of subsidy funds, such as automatically matching service providers for caregiving subsidies for disabled elderly individuals.

(3) **Data Elements and Risk Control: Constructing a Dynamic Defense System**

Data-driven risk control models are increasingly replacing traditional rule engines. By collecting comprehensive lifecycle data of insured individuals (including employment, medical, and credit records) and applying gradient boosting algorithms such as XGBoost and LightGBM, multi-dimensional risk evaluation matrices can be constructed. For example, the system can identify fraudulent risks in patterns of "interrupted contributions and re-enrollment" by using clustering analysis to differentiate normal employment fluctuations from deliberate fraudulent behavior. The development of regulatory technology (RegTech) has translated pension regulatory rules into algorithmic logic—known as "Regulatory Code"—enabling real-time monitoring of fund balances and automatically generating compliance reports; for example, if a region's pension replacement rate drops abnormally, the system immediately initiates a stress test and issues an early warning.

(4) **RegTech: Establishing a New Paradigm for Collaborative Governance**

Financial regulatory authorities are piloting innovative applications of AI in the pension sector through "regulatory sandbox" mechanisms. The National Financial Supervision Administration has called for "strengthening the full-process security management of AI technologies," requiring financial institutions to establish a comprehensive regulatory framework covering data collection, model training, and decision output. For example, in intelligent investment advisory systems, each algorithmic decision must be recorded with its underlying basis (including the sources of training data and the distribution of feature weights) to ensure traceability; simultaneously, adversarial sample testing is conducted to verify model stability under extreme market conditions, thereby preventing systemic risks in pension investment portfolios. The "FantaiKe" Fintech Competition in Beijing's Zhongguancun has designated RegTech as a key track to promote the deep integration of AI with pension regulation.

6.1.4 Technological Integration and Addressing Challenges

The integration of artificial intelligence and fintech exhibits a "mutual empowerment" characteristic: on one hand, financial scenarios provide rich application environments (such as pension actuarial models and asset allocation) that drive iterative technological advancements; on the other hand, AI technologies resolve pain points in financial services, such as enhancing pension management efficiency and improving risk prevention capabilities. However, significant challenges remain, including balancing data privacy protection with data utilization, addressing fairness issues arising from algorithmic biases, and mitigating regulatory challenges posed by the "black box" nature of technologies. To address these, it is necessary to establish a "technology-institution" collaborative framework: at the technical level, invest in privacy-enhancing technologies such as federated learning and secure multi-party computation; at the institutional level, refine AI ethics guidelines and regulatory rules, drawing on systems like the EU's Artificial Intelligence Act's risk classification, which could serve as a reference for AI applications in the pension sector.

Looking ahead, with the deepening application of embodied AI, unified multimodal large models, and intelligent agents, pension management will progress towards a new phase characterized by precision, personalization, and automation. The core of technological development lies in consistently addressing the sustainability challenges posed by population aging, enhancing institutional resilience through innovation, and striking a dynamic balance between efficiency gains and risk prevention, thereby providing robust technological support for a multi-layered, multi-pillar pension system.

6.2 AI+ in Personal Pension Services

6.2.1 Intelligent Investment Advisory and Personalized Services: A Data-Driven Revolution in Retirement Wealth Management

Intelligent investment advisory systems integrate multidimensional user data with machine learning algorithms to build dynamic allocation models that span the entire life cycle. In accordance with the 2025 "Personal Pension Implementation Measures," such systems must collect over 200 features—including age, occupation, income fluctuations, and health status—to form differentiated retirement needs profiles. For example, the "Retirement Planning Calculator" from Construction Bank, trained on data from 230 million clients using an XGBoost model, can generate a three-tier scheme that covers basic reserves, annuity allocation, and risk hedging. This model tailors for 35-year-old white-collar workers, achieving precise matching between expected annual returns and risk tolerance, with an error margin controlled within 5%.

In the stage of product matching, the AI system uses natural language processing to parse regulatory policies and automatically select compliant financial products. For instance, Taikang Life Insurance's "Yi Yang You Yue" annuity product is algorithmically configured to allocate 50% of assets to low-risk government bonds, 30% to dividend-based insurance products, and reserve 20% for dynamic adjustments, thus fulfilling the dual requirements of "long-term annuity functionality plus a capital safety cushion" stipulated in the "Commercial Insurance Annuity Notice," and its robustness under interest rate fluctuations has been validated via Monte Carlo simulations, with a historical maximum drawdown of less than 3%. For high-net-worth clients, the system supports the integration of personal pension accounts with family trusts through smart contracts to achieve coordinated wealth transfer and pension protection, having already served more than 200 high-value families.

6.2.2 *Risk Management and Compliance Monitoring: An End-To-End Defense System Constructed by Algorithms*

AI risk control systems integrate multisource data from social security, finance, and judicial records to construct three-dimensional evaluation models for behavioral, market, and operational risks. For example, the "No Proof of Social Security" platform in Tai'an, Shandong, employs graph neural networks to identify abnormal contribution patterns—such as "three instances of large cross-provincial supplementary contributions within six months combined with abnormal fund flows"—achieving a model accuracy rate of 92% and successfully intercepting 127 suspected fraud cases in 2024. In the realm of data security, the Federated Learning technology developed by the Guangdong Anzheng Forensic Institute supports cross-institution data sharing by transmitting only encrypted feature vectors, ensuring raw data remains local. This technology has been applied in risk control model training by 15 financial institutions, in compliance with the "Measures for the Security Assessment of Data Outflows."

The integration of regulatory rules into algorithmic systems accomplishes a proactive approach to compliance management. The system converts the 127 indicators in the 2025 "Personal Information Protection Compliance Audit Management Measures" into code logic to automatically scan products before launch. For instance, a "High-Yield Annuity" product from an insurance company, which advertised "guaranteed returns," was intercepted for violating Article 25 of the Advertising Law. A stress test mechanism for extreme scenarios can simulate 12 different conditions—such as a lifespan extension to 95 years or a 3% GDP contraction—and automatically trigger asset rebalancing when a portfolio loss exceeds 15%; historical testing shows this can reduce potential risks by 18%.

6.2.3 *Enhanced Operational Efficiency and Optimized Customer Experience: Technology Reshaping the Service Ecosystem*

AI technology has driven personal pension services to achieve the "three reductions and two increases": reducing materials, steps, and time, while increasing efficiency and user experience. For example, the "Digital Social Security Employee" system implemented by Tai'an Municipality's Human Resources and Social Security Bureau uses RPA robots to process work injury benefit audits, reducing the processing time per case from 20 to 4 min; in 2024, it processed 120,000 transactions with a 100% accuracy rate. In the area of intelligent account opening, Construction Bank's "facial recognition + OCR" technology has shortened the process to 1 min, and the integration of electronic certificate systems has enabled "proof-free" procedures, serving over 1.5 million users in the first quarter of 2025—an 85% improvement in efficiency.

For the elderly, adaptive modifications have been applied to optimize multimodal interactions. The "Care Mode" in Construction Bank's mobile banking app supports recognition of 21 dialects, achieving a 98% accuracy rate for voice queries regarding account balances among elderly users, and provides policy interpretation videos in dialects. Taiping Insurance's "Retirement Planning Cockpit" features a graphical interface that highlights key data (such as contribution shortfalls and investment returns) with contrasting colors and is supported by video customer service for real-time guidance, increasing the success rate of elderly users from 35 to 68%. In offline settings, Tai'an communities have deployed "AI Teller Machines" that integrate 106 social security services and, through the sharing of electronic certificates, enable 15 services to be processed "zero-materially;" in 2024, these machines covered 83% of all streets.

6.2.4 *Policy Support and Product Innovation: The Synergistic Evolution of Institutions and Technology*

AI systems leverage digital policy parsing to enable the precise implementation of institutional innovations. For example, in response to Shandong's "Talent Annuity" policy, the system automatically identifies six types of talent—including Taishan Scholars—and generates customized schemes and supports batch account openings for enterprises; by 2025, it had served 12,000 industrial park enterprises, increasing the talent annuity coverage rate to 45%. In the application of tax incentives, the system automatically calculates the annual tax-preferred allowance for users with an annual salary of 200,000 yuan (i.e., 2,400 yuan), and 30 days prior to individual income tax filing, pushes a "Policy Package" that includes the generation of payment vouchers and filing guidelines, achieving a reach rate of 96%.

Technology-driven product innovations are increasingly characterized by scenario-specific and green features. For instance, Construction Bank's "Education and Pension Dual Account" dynamically allocates funds via algorithms—allocating 60% of funds to education for children under 18 and increasing pension reserves to 80% after 18—to achieve comprehensive household financial management. Taikang Insurance's "Carbon Neutral Pension Annuity", which is linked to green bonds, uses AI to monitor real-time carbon reductions (e.g., exchanging a 10-ton CO_2 reduction per year for caregiving services), thus attracting a shift in investor composition, with the share of investors under 35 rising to 32%. In the realm of regulatory technology, the national personal pension risk monitoring platform utilizes AI to analyze over two million transaction records; if a region's replacement rate declines by more than 5% for three consecutive months, it automatically generates an early warning report containing 12 remedial measures—successfully predicting three regional risks in 2024.

6.3 Implementation Pathways for AI Empowerment in the Personal Pension Industry Development

6.3.1 Technology-Driven: Constructing a Comprehensive Digital Infrastructure Along the Industrial Chain

(1) **Construction of Quantitative and Standardized Longevity Risk Systems**

In response to the longevity risk management challenges raised by Committee Member Sun Jie of the Financial Times, AI technology must establish a standardized mortality prediction framework. In March 2025, the Ministry of Human Resources and Social Security and the Financial Regulatory Administration initiated the "China Longevity Index" development project, which employs machine learning algorithms to dynamically forecast survival probabilities across different regions, genders, and age cohorts, utilizing data from social security, healthcare, and insurance sectors. For instance, the pilot platform in Zhejiang Province has integrated health data from 120 million insured individuals, achieving a prediction error rate of less than 3% for the remaining life expectancy of seniors over 70 through an XGBoost model, thereby providing a scientific basis for annuity product pricing. This index system, scheduled for official release in 2026, will serve as the core pricing benchmark for longevity risk securitization.

(2) **Upgrading the Life-Cycle Account Management System**

According to the joint "Notice" issued by five governmental departments in December 2024, personal pension accounts must facilitate "one-time registration with nationwide validity." The AI system achieves real-time integration between social security accounts and fund accounts through a unified identity authentication interface. For example, the Industrial and Commercial Bank of China's "e-Pension" platform employs federated learning technology to integrate 18 dimensions of data—including social security contributions, investment returns, and healthcare expenditures—while preserving user privacy, thereby generating personalized pension reserve heat maps. Users can visualize account balance trajectories across different life stages through an augmented reality interface and simulate benefit levels by adjusting parameters such as retirement age via interactive sliders.

(3) **Age-Friendly Modification of Intelligent Terminals and Scenario Extension**

The Ministry of Civil Affairs' report on "Artificial Intelligence + Facilitating New Developments in Pension Services "emphasizes the need to accelerate the development of age-friendly intelligent terminals. The "AI Social Security Kiosk" piloted in Tai'an has incorporated biometric recognition features, supporting multi-factor authentication including fingerprints and iris scans, reducing operation error rates among elderly users to 12%. Concurrently, in conjunction with the early withdrawal scenarios newly added in the "Notice," the system integrates critical illness data from medical insurance systems to automatically activate expedited approval channels for patients with cancer and 24 other diseases. The 2025 new terminal model has realized an integrated "facial recognition, voice operation, and remote assistance" service paradigm, with a rural coverage rate reaching 85%.

6.3.2 Institutional Coordination: Creating Bidirectional Empowerment Mechanisms Between Policy and Technology

(1) **Intelligent Tax Incentive Adaptation System**

Interfacing with the nationally unified personal pension information management service platform, the AI system automatically identifies users' income levels and matches them with optimal tax incentive schemes. For instance, for salaried employees with monthly incomes of 8,000 yuan, the system recommends an "annual lump-sum contribution + salary deduction" model, enhancing tax efficiency by 35%; self-employed individuals can opt for "quarterly flexible contributions," with the system dynamically adjusting contribution amounts based on business revenue flows, ensuring full utilization of tax incentives. As of January 2025, 32 million users nationwide have received tax incentive reminders via the intelligent system, raising policy coverage to 92%.

(2) **Regulatory Sandbox Mechanism for Product Innovation**

Addressing the "product homogenization" issue raised by Committee Member Sun Jie, regulatory authorities have established a "Pension FinTech Sandbox," permitting pilot testing of AI-driven innovative products. For example, a life-cycle target fund developed by a fund company dynamically adjusts the allocation ratio of equity assets by analyzing users' career trajectories (e.g., programmers, teachers) through multimodal large language models. Sandbox testing demonstrated that the product reduced long-term return volatility by 18%, and by March 2025, it had obtained regulatory approval for formal distribution to the 35–50 age demographic.

(3) **Compliance Framework for Data Element Circulation**

In accordance with the Personal Information Protection Law, a sharing mechanism that ensures "data usability without visibility" has been constructed. Zhejiang's Social Security-Financial Data Coordination Platform employs zero-knowledge proof technology, enabling financial institutions to verify users' contribution capacity without accessing raw data. For instance, a bank can query a user's social security contribution base for the preceding three years through this platform. Combined with an AI credit scoring model, the system recommends appropriate pension savings products, achieving a 100% data usage compliance rate. The platform processes an average of 230,000 cross-institutional query requests daily, supporting 45% of the province's personal pension transaction processing.

6.3.3 Industrial Ecosystem: Cultivating Diversified AI + Pension Service Clusters

(1) **Financial Innovation for Longevity Risk Hedging**

Drawing on the pilot experience of the Shanghai Insurance Exchange, AI systems have developed "longevity risk swap contracts." Insurance companies collect survival data from tens of millions of individuals to train mortality prediction models, packaging longevity risk into financial derivatives. For example, Taikang Insurance's "Longevity Risk ABS" automatically matches retirement community residency rights with policy benefits through smart contracts; when actual longevity exceeds projections, capital market investors share the excess payment burden. By the first quarter of 2025, this product had reached a scale of 12 billion yuan, covering 500,000 elderly users.

(2) **Scenario-Based Services for Industrial Coordination**

In conjunction with the "Specific Pension Savings" product newly added in the "Notice," AI systems have created a "savings + services" ecosystem. Construction Bank's "Pension Wallet" integrates over 2,000 service providers covering community dining, health management, and other services. After users redeem services using pension points, the system automatically analyzes consumption patterns to adjust investment strategies. For example, for users who frequently utilize traditional Chinese medicine therapeutic services, the system increases allocations to health management insurance products, forming a "savings-consumption-protection" closed loop. Data from 2025 indicates that this model's user retention rate exceeds that of traditional products by 27%.

(3) **Precision Service Networks for Vulnerable Groups**

For low-income groups, AI systems have developed "principal-protected + variable" return products. For instance, "Warm Heart Pension Treasure" offers a 2.5% guaranteed return, with excess returns distributed according to investment performance, while management fees have been reduced to 0.1%. The system automatically identifies eligible users through integration with civil affairs minimum living allowance data, promoting a "contribution first, subsidy later" policy (e.g., a 50-yuan government subsidy for a 1,000-yuan contribution). Implementation of this model in pilot regions of Guizhou has increased rural participation rates from 18 to 43%, with per capita pension reserves rising by 12,000 yuan.

6.3.4 Risk Response: Constructing a Resilient Full-Chain Protection System

(1) **Algorithmic Fairness Governance Framework**

An "AI Pension Decision-Making Committee" has been established, inviting elderly representatives, regulatory authorities, and technical experts to participate in algorithm reviews. To address the low model adaptation rate for rural residents, Tencent's FinTech team has added feature dimensions such as "land transfer income" and "grain subsidies," enhancing model generalization capabilities through generative adversarial networks (GANs). Tests in March 2025 demonstrated that risk assessment accuracy for rural users increased from 78 to 94%, while urban–rural strategy disparity decreased to 5%.

(2) **Technology-Enabled Dynamic Regulation**

The national personal pension risk monitoring platform has been upgraded to an "Intelligent Regulatory Brain," employing graph neural networks to identify anomalous transaction patterns. For example, when a payment agency concentrated on opening accounts for 200 individuals with substantial deposits in a short period, the system automatically flagged this as high-risk; subsequent verification in coordination with public security departments uncovered tax fraud cases, recovering losses exceeding 8 million yuan. The platform processes an average of 1,200 risk alerts daily, reducing risk identification latency from T + 3 days to T + 1 hour.

(3) **Compliance Sandbox for Technological Iteration**

A "Pension AI Innovation Laboratory" has been established, allowing enterprises to test frontier technologies such as embodied intelligence customer service and brain-computer interface terminals. For instance, Xiaomi's "Pension Companion Robot" employs affective computing to recognize user emotions, automatically switching to slower speech rates and multi-case study modes when explaining investment risks, improving elderly user acceptance by 60%. The laboratory has formulated 12 age-friendly technical standards, including voice interaction delays not exceeding 0.5 s and interface fonts not smaller than size 24, ensuring synchronized enhancement of technological innovation and user experience.

6.3.5 *Future Outlook: Constructing a New Smart Pension Industrial Ecosystem*

With the deepening implementation of the "14th Five-Year Plan for National Aging Development," AI empowerment of personal pensions will exhibit three major industrial trends:

(1) **Vertical Integration of the Industrial Chain**

From account management to benefit reception, a full-chain closed loop of "data collection—risk assessment—product adaptation—service extension" is forming. For example, Ping An Group's "Smart Pension Ecosystem" integrates insurance, healthcare, and community services, enabling users to complete comprehensive processes including pension investment, health management, and retirement community reservations through a single application.

(2) **Cross-Boundary Technological Convergence**

Brain-computer interface technology is being applied to care for disabled elderly individuals, while AR technology is reconstructing pension education scenarios. Tianjin University's "AR Pension Planning Sandbox" allows users to simulate returns under different contribution schemes through gesture operations, enhancing decision-making efficiency by 40%.

(3) **Global Collaborative Innovation**

Drawing on international experience, Shanghai will establish an "Asia–Pacific Longevity Risk Trading Center," utilizing blockchain technology to achieve cross-border risk hedging. By 2027, China's pension financial derivatives market is projected to exceed 500 billion yuan, providing a "Chinese solution" for global aging governance.

The essence of industrial development lies in resolving institutional pain points through technological innovation and activating market potential through data elements. When longevity risk becomes quantifiable, products and services customizable, and regulatory rules computable, personal pensions will evolve from singular savings instruments into core hubs connecting financial markets, the real economy, and public services. This pathway requires multi-stakeholder coordination among government, enterprises, and society to realize technological dividends while ensuring data security, ultimately constructing a new smart pension ecosystem covering 1.4 billion people and providing sustainable industrial solutions for addressing deep population aging.

MIX
Papier aus verantwortungsvollen Quellen
Paper from responsible sources
FSC® C105338

If you have any concerns about our products,
you can contact us on
ProductSafety@springernature.com

In case Publisher is established outside the EU,
the EU authorized representative is:
Springer Nature Customer Service Center GmbH
Europaplatz 3, 69115 Heidelberg, Germany

Printed by Libri Plureos GmbH
in Hamburg, Germany